THE KIDS' GUIDE TO
Digital Photography

SARAH SMITH

for participating in a
Photography Workshop
Summer Reading Program
2009

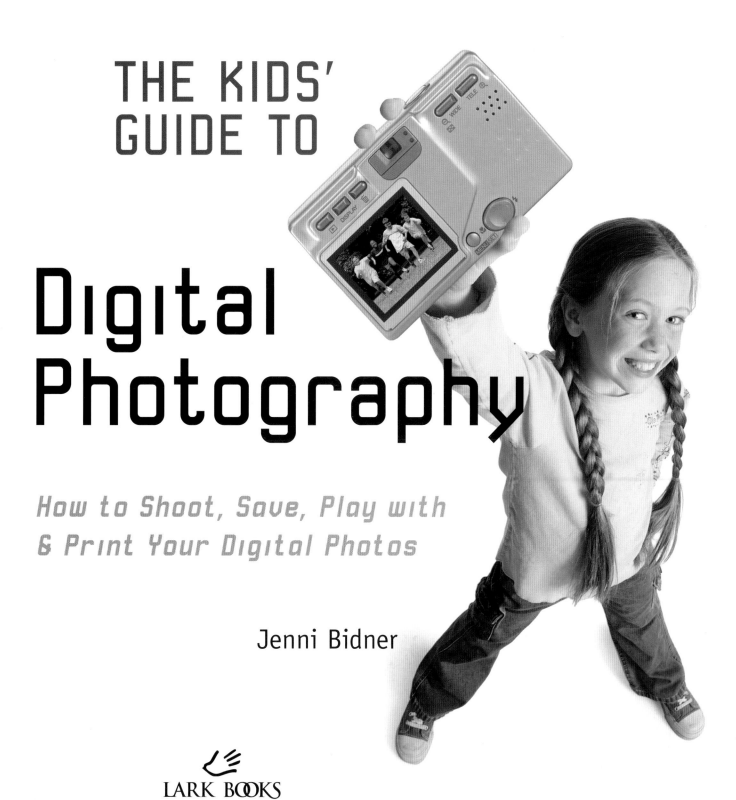

THE KIDS'
GUIDE TO

Digital
Photography

How to Shoot, Save, Play with
& Print Your Digital Photos

Jenni Bidner

LARK BOOKS

A Division of Sterling Publishing Co., Inc.
New York / London

EDITOR
Joe Rhatigan

SENIOR ART DIRECTOR
Chris Bryant

DESIGNER
Jenni Bidner

PHOTOGRAPHER
Jenni Bidner

COVER DESIGNER
Barbara Zaretsky

ASSOCIATE EDITOR
Rain Newcomb

EDITORIAL ASSISTANCE
Delores Gosnell

PRODUCTION ASSISTANCE
Shannon Yokeley

PROJECT DESIGNERS

Suzanne Tourtillott: Pages
66, 85, 86, 90, 92, and 93

Pamela Smart: Pages 84, 87,
88, and 91

SPECIAL PHOTOGRAPHY CREDITS

Steve Mann: Pages 66
and 84 through 93

© Meleda Wegner:
Author photo

© Eric Bean: Pages 5, 64, and 73

Sandra Stambaugh: Pages 10,
28 (top), 30, 31 (top), 47
(bottom right), 48 (top)

John Widman: Page 48
(bottom right)

Wolf on pages 12 and 13
photographed at the
Wildlife Science Center,
www.wildlifesciencecenter.org

The Library of Congress has cataloged the hardcover edition as follows:

Bidner, Jenni.
 The kids' guide to digital photography : how to shoot, save, play with & print your
digital photos / Jenni Bidner.
     p. cm.
 Includes index.
 ISBN 1-57990-604-4 (hardcover)
 1. Photography--Digital techniques--Juvenile literature. I. Title.
TR267.B546 2004
775--dc22

                                                                    2004014465

10 9 8 7 6 5 4

Published by Lark Books, a division of
Sterling Publishing Co., Inc.
387 Park Avenue South, New York, N.Y. 10016

First Paperback Edition 2005
© 2004, Jenni Bidner

Distributed in Canada by Sterling Publishing,
c/o Canadian Manda Group, 165 Dufferin Street
Toronto, Ontario, Canada M6K 3H6

Distributed in the United Kingdom by GMC Distribution Services,
Castle Place, 166 High Street, Lewes, East Sussex, England BN7 1XU

Distributed in Australia by Capricorn Link (Australia) Pty Ltd.,
P.O. Box 704, Windsor, NSW 2756 Australia

If you have questions or comments about this book, please contact:
Lark Books, 67 Broadway, Asheville, NC 28801, (828) 253-0467

Manufactured in China

ISBN 13: 978-1-57990-604-7 (hardcover) 978-1-57990-643-6 (paperback)

For information about custom editions, special sales, premium and corporate purchases, please
contact Sterling Special Sales Department at 800-805-5489 or specialsales@sterlingpub.com.

Contents

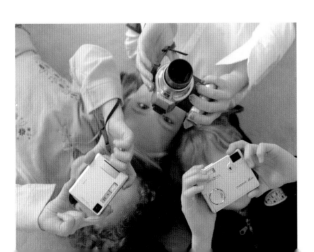

Introduction

DIGITAL PHOTOGRAPHY IS A LOT EASIER THAN YOU THINK!

It's easier than photography with film, because you know instantly whether you got the shot or not. And it's a ton more fun because you can share your cool results with friends just seconds after you take a picture.

But what about the computer side? Well, if you can play games on your computer, then you have just about all the skills you need to get started with a digital camera. All you're really doing is taking a picture with a mini-computer (your camera) and transferring it to your desktop or laptop computer. Once on your computer, you can save it, copy it, or transform it into a new artistic creation.

Best yet, you can shoot, and shoot, and shoot, and shoot—and never have to spend a dime on film and processing. Paper and ink cost money, but when your allowance runs out, you can always share your pictures through emails (free!) and maybe even your own website.

So, what exactly does digital photography involve? Well, that's what this book is all about. But for a jump-start, you can turn to the Ten Steps to Success on pages 9 and 10 to see how easy "going digital" really is. Then try some of the neat techniques for taking great pictures. You can even turn your awesome pictures into cool crafts, gifts, and other fun stuff. But most of all, go out and enjoy your camera.

With this book, you'll be able to...

- Figure out everything you need to get started taking digital pictures

- Find out what kind of digital camera is best for you

- Use terms like "jpeg" and "megapixel" with a confidence that will make your parents jealous

- Save your pictures so that they're the right size for emailing, printing, and putting on your website

- Turn your scanner into a camera

- Find out how all those little buttons on your camera work

- Take great pictures of friends, pets, vacation spots, sports action, and even yourself

- Borrow techniques from the pros to make your pictures even better

- Manipulate your photos on your computer to make them look better or just plain wacky

- Post images on your website

- Make awesome prints that look just as good as regular film photographs

- Create cool things, such as cards, bookplates, pet portraits, and more using your digital photographs

1

Digital Basics

Most digital cameras are so easy to use, you can just pick them up and start shooting good pictures. But a few digital topics, such as resolution, are important to understand if you want really good shots.

What's a Digital Picture?

A digital picture is simply a photo that has been converted into "computer language" and saved as a file. A digital camera takes pictures without film. You can also use a scanner to convert prints and film into digital pictures.

Once on your computer, you can open the picture file and the computer displays the picture. Just like most other computer files, a digital picture file can be saved on your hard drive, as well as on a recordable CD. It can be attached to an email and sent over the Internet, or posted to your website (see chapter 5).

You can alter or play with your digital photos, and then print them onto special paper so they look just like the prints you'd get from a photo lab. And finally, you can use specialty papers to turn your pictures into great crafts and projects (see chapter 7).

Ten Steps to Success

Digital photography can sound scary, but it's not. It's really just plain old regular photography, except instead of film, the camera takes the picture on computer memory. Here's the whole process. from start to finish in 10 easy steps:

1 LOAD MEMORY INTO YOUR CAMERA

Load the camera with a memory card or memory stick. This is the digital equivalent of film. (A few older or cheap digital cameras don't have removable memory.)

2 ERASE OLD MEMORY

Format the memory card or stick so there are no pictures on it. But wait! If there are pictures that you want to keep, you'll need to transfer them to the computer first (see step 6) or you'll lose them forever!

3 SET RESOLUTION (PICTURE SIZE)

Select the resolution or picture size you want. In average situations, with a camera that shoots low resolution email-sized files, you can hold over 160 on a 16 MB card or over 600 on a 64 MB card.

High resolution pictures on a three or four megapixel camera will eat up memory a lot faster, creating files that are 2 MB or more apiece, meaning 32 or fewer pictures on a 64 MB card (see pages 11 to 13 for more details).

4 SHOOT GREAT PICTURES!

It works just like a film camera. See chapters 3 and 4 for shooting tips.

5 TRANSFER TO COMPUTER

Download the images to your computer. This can be done by connecting the camera to the computer (with a cord or wireless), or by removing the memory card or stick and putting it in a reader. It's usually pretty easy to do, but read your instruction manual if you have trouble.

6 SAVE THE PICTURES

Transfer or save these pictures into a folder. Use the default folder (such as "my pictures") or create your own special folder.

7 OPEN & EDIT PICTURES

Open the pictures on your computer with photo-editing software. Delete the bad pictures. Keep the good ones.

8 ERASE OR CLEAR MEMORY

Once you're sure the good pictures have been transferred to the computer, erase the memory card or stick. This command is called erase, format, or reformat. It can be done with the computer or with the camera.

9 BACKUP (COPY) PICTURES

Since there are no negatives, the file on the computer is now the only record of the picture. You may accidentally delete the image, or it could be erased if the computer crashes. Therefore it is a good idea to backup the best images, by making a copy on a CD, Zip disk, or other removable media.

10 GO OUT AND SHOOT SOME MORE PICTURES!

Don't worry if you don't know how to do all these steps. I'll take you through them in the rest of the book!

A Big Jigsaw Puzzle

A digital picture is like a big, finished jigsaw puzzle. But instead of puzzle pieces, it's made up of PIXELS. Each PIXEL holds a little piece of the picture on it, just like a jigsaw piece. When they're all lined up and in the right place, you can suddenly see the whole picture!

The more pieces (PIXELS) you have, the bigger the jigsaw picture can be. A camera that can shoot one MEGAPIXEL, means the picture has 1,000,000 *(one million!)* pieces. And five megapixels means five million pixels.

The number of pixels in a picture is also called its RESOLUTION. High-resolution images have more pixels, while low-resolution have fewer. Because a high-resolution picture has more pixels (more puzzle pieces), it takes more memory to save it in the camera and on the computer. In other words, it has a bigger FILE SIZE.

Resolutions

Most digital cameras give you a choice of what RESOLUTION (picture size or pixel size) to set before shooting your pictures. *So what's better? High or low resolution?*

Well, bigger is usually better, because a high resolution (two, three, four and five megapixels) picture means it will look really great when you blow it up into a big print. And while a low-resolution picture has a small file size (so it emails quickly), you can't print it big and hope to get nice quality.

It's sometimes hard to predict if that silly snapshot might become your all-time favorite photo, so when in doubt, play it safe and shoot at the highest or second highest resolution.

THE BIG BUT

Unfortunately, there are a few disadvantages to high resolution pictures. It takes longer for your camera to process the picture, which can lead to delays before the camera is "ready" to take the next picture.

The file size of a high-resolution photograph is much bigger than a low resolution picture. This means it will take more space in your computer's hard drive (it will take up more memory). It will also take longer to OPEN and SAVE in photo-editing or other software.

Worst yet, if you try to email a high-resolution picture, it could seem to take forever for the recipient to receive it, and it may appear huge on their monitor, requiring them to SCROLL to see the full picture.

resolution just right

resolution is too low

Resolution Solution

HIGH RES = BEST QUALITY + BIG PRINTS
LOW RES = FAST EMAILS + LOTS MORE PICTURES

How Big Is the Big Bad Wolf?

You're at the zoo taking pictures for the field-trip report. What resolution should you set?

If your camera only has one resolution setting, your choice is easy. But most digital cameras have two, three, or even more choices.

Now it's a tough call! If you go with the highest resolution, you may only be able to shoot a few pictures before all the memory in your camera is filled. But those pictures will be great quality, and you can blow them up to make HUGE posters. Or you can crop out a lot of the background and still have enough pixels for a good print. (See pages 54, 55, or 61 for more information on cropping.)

On the other hand, if you shoot low resolution, you can take dozens and dozens of pic-tures without running out of memory. The more you shoot, the better chance you have of getting that one-in-a-million shot that will have all your friends going "oooh" and "ahhhh." But since they're low resolution, they won't print as well. They'll probably look great as email attachments or on the school website, but when printed in your report or for a wall display, the quality will go way down.

Before you make a decision, count up how many different kinds of shots you need for the project. Be generous in your count. This is the absolute minimum number of shots you need to come home with. Then add a few to the account for pictures of friends and fun stuff.

Just like a film camera counts down how many shots you have before you get to the end of the roll, a digital camera gives you a number as well. Check the information panel on the top of the camera when you have it set at a low resolution (small picture size), and you'll see a much higher number of shots than when you set it to a higher resolution (bigger picture size).

At the highest resolution are there at least as many frames as you need? If so, start shooting, and then use the MONITOR and PLAYBACK to edit as you go, so you can DELETE the bad pictures.

If not, reduce the resolution setting until the number of frames listed on the information panel matches the minimum number of photos you need.

Resolution Math!

As I mentioned before, the actual size of a digital image is usually stated in pixels, and the total number of pixels is its resolution. Resolution can be stated as a single number, such as 1,000,000 (one million or one MEGAPIXEL).

Resolution can also be stated as a math expression, such as 300x450 pixels (pronounced 300 "by" 450 pixels). This means the picture is 300 pixels wide, by 450 pixels long.

Surprise! Math quiz! The total number of pixels would be 300 times 450, or 135,000 pixels, because:

$$300 \times 450 = 135,000$$

Instead of having to write out a lot of zeroes, digital camera makers decided on the term megapixel to mean one million (1,000,000) pixels. Therefore a one megapixel camera can shoot pictures that are about 800x1200 resolution, because:

$$800 \times 1200 = 960,000$$

It's not uncommon to see five MEGAPIXELS (with a whopping 5,000,000 pixels) in a point-and-shoot camera.

JPEG File Formats

Most cameras shoot pictures in the JPEG file format, though some offer additional choices such as TIFF and RAW. Once in the computer any of these formats can be resaved into different file formats.

A JPEG file has a file name that ends with ".jpg" (note in some Mac and Windows programs, these letters may be invisible). JPEG is a good format for photos because it can show millions of colors, and therefore looks realistic.

It's also popular because it's a COMPRESSION file format that can be reduced to one-tenth the normal file size with little loss of detail. Compressed files take up less memory so you can shoot more before you need to DOWNLOAD (transfer) them to your computer.

MORE ON COMPRESSION

Compression comes with a price. As you make the file size smaller (COMPRESS the image), you will start to see a loss of detail and the picture will start to look bad.

The good news is that you generally can't see the difference until you start getting quite small (HIGH COMPRESSION). Medium to high quality (LOW to MEDIUM COMPRESSION) is okay for most photos.

Some cameras offer different compression options when shooting pictures. For the best results, select low compression (bigger file size and fewer shots per memory card or memory stick). In the computer, the COMPRESSION can also be increased to make a file smaller for emailing.

The COMPRESSION option usually appears in a PREVIEW window when you use the SAVE or

SAVE AS function in photo-editing software. Make sure the PREVIEW box is clicked, so you can watch the quality change. Continue compressing the image until you see a change in quality, then go up one or two levels in quality.

Other File Formats

If you receive email pictures or download images from a website, they may be GIF or BMP (bitmap) formats. These are two older file formats. Their only big advantage is their extremely small file size. The pictures don't always look good, because they are made up of too few colors.

Because website owners want you to be able to view their sites quickly, this smaller size is an advantage (GIF and BMP pictures

take very little time to download). Therefore you'll often see them on the Internet.

The TIFF format is a high-quality format, primarily used for professional printing and photographic applications and retouching. Some high-end cameras will shoot TIFF images. The files it creates are huge, because there is no COMPRESSION. For most home purposes, JPEG is a better choice.

If you're having trouble sharing pictures with your friends, RESAVE the photo as a JPEG. Usually this in done inside a PHOTO-EDITING software program, by going to the FILE command and then RESAVE command. Be sure you've named this new picture, so you don't ERASE the old higher resolution file.

HOW MANY MEGAPIXELS SHOULD MY CAMERA BE?

A megapixel equals one million (1,000,000) pixels. It sounds like a lot, but a one-megapixel camera is actually considered a very low-resolution camera these days—if you can even find one!

■ **UNDER 3 MEGAPIXELS:** This camera is good for photo to use for email, websites, and small prints.

■ **3 MEGAPIXELS:** All of the above, plus nice photo-quality prints (from home or a lab) up to 8x10-inch, 11x14-inch, or even larger.

■ **4+ MEGAPIXELS:** Even after cropping the image (see page 61), you can make large beautiful prints.

Choosing a Camera

Whether you're about to buy a camera, you have a great new one, or you're "stuck" using the family camera, you'll need to know what your camera can do. Not all the features mentioned in chapter 2 are available on simpler cameras, and the big, bulky professional-style cameras have a lot of complicated controls.

There are numerous types of digital cameras, ranging from ultra-simple low resolution models, to professional cameras costing thousands of dollars. The most common is the point-and-shoot style, but you can also get SLR cameras, or personal entertainment devices that merge pictures with MP3 music or cell phones.

Is Begging for a Digital Camera Not Working?

IMPRESS YOUR PARENTS WITH YOUR MATH SKILLS!

Do the math: Figure out the cost of one film roll plus processing, then multiply by the number of rolls the family shoots in a year. Your parents may be surprised how quickly you can "pay off" your new camera in savings. Of course, you'll need to consider the cost of inkjet paper and supplies for prints, but you'll find you don't print every image—just the very best.

POINT-AND-SHOOT

Point-and-shoot digital cameras are exactly what they sound like. You point, you shoot, and you usually get pretty good pictures.

Some point-and-shoot cameras offer many advanced features like specialized EXPOSURE MODES, while others are no-frills. They range for simple pictures, to megapixel models offering resolutions over 8 million pixels (see pages 10 to 13).

Point-and-shoot cameras are designed to be easy to use. Some really are, while others may seem very confusing with a dizzying number of controls. If you're skilled with a film camera, you should have no trouble with any digital camera.

DIGITAL SLR CAMERAS

Unless one of your parents is a photo-geek, you probably won't have a digital SLR (single-lens reflex) camera. They are big and bulky, and most have fancy lenses that can be removed and changed. *But wow!* Can they take some amazing pictures if you take the time to learn how to use them. Unfortunately, they're also pretty expensive, so if you wreck it, we could be talking about allowance or babysitting money for the next 10 years!

PICTURE-PHONES & MORE

Some cell phones, MP3 players, and other personal entertainment devices have built-in cameras or camera attachments. Most don't offer the control and advanced capabilities of a regular digital camera, but they can be a lot of fun to use.

Many digital camcorders (DV) can also take still digital pictures. Again, check and see if the camera you're considering offers some of the advanced controls mentioned later in this book if you plan on making it your only digital camera.

Zoom point-and-shoot

Cool Camera Features

If you've been shopping for digital cameras, you've certainly noticed that there are a lot of features to consider. The next four pages detail some of the most important features. chapter 2 discusses in detail how to use many of them. And the chart on pages 20 and 21 can help you quickly decide which you really want or need.

Point-and-shoot with rotating monitor

CONNECTION TYPE

The first step is to check compatibility. Can your camera (and the software that comes with it) work on your computer? Check to see if the operating system (such as Windows or Mac OSX) is listed on the camera box.

The camera will probably have a connection port for hooking it up to the computer when you want to DOWNLOAD your pictures. This port must match your computer. USB and FIREWIRE are good ports for transferring information between computer and camera.

If your camera has removable memory cards or sticks, you can hook up a card reader (instead of the camera) to the computer.

Digital SLR

DV camcorder that also shoots still pictures

FIXED OR ZOOM LENS?

The lens on your digital camera is very important. Some cameras have a FIXED LENS, meaning you look through the viewfinder and see the scene. Then to get a wider view of the scene, you'd have to step back. To get a closer look, you'd need to step forward.

A ZOOM lens is much better, because you can change the view just by zooming the lens from WIDE (W) to TELE (T). It's not too much different from picking up a pair of binoculars to get a closer look at a distant baseball player.

Not only is this convenient, but there will be times when you wouldn't want to step backwards or forwards—just imagine taking pictures on the edge of the Grand Canyon, and you'll know what I mean!

What is MB?

MB is a megabyte, which equals 1000 kilobytes (k). It's just a number that represents how much computer memory a file takes, or its file size.

A 64 MB memory card has four times (4X) as much memory space as a 16 MB card. A 2 MB file (2000K) is 100 times bigger than a 20K file.

ALL ZOOMS ARE NOT THE SAME

Zoom lenses vary from camera to camera in two ways. The first is how wide or how close they can get you. For the greatest range of choices, look for one that lists the biggest zoom range. For example, a 4X zoom has a greater range than a 2X zoom.

Sometimes zoom lenses are described as a "35mm film format equivalent," such as 35mm–105mm. The bigger the difference between these numbers, the better the zoom range (35mm–135mm is a better range than 35mm–70mm).

The second difference is OPTICAL ZOOM versus DIGITAL ZOOM, and it's night and day between the two! OPTICAL ZOOM is much, much better. It gets you a closer look at your subject without reducing the resolution or the image quality.

If you use DIGITAL ZOOM, you will sacrifice quality and resolution! In fact, if your camera offers digital zoom, I recommend going into the control or settings menu (see the instruction manual) and turning it off.

VIEWFINDERS & MONITORS

Most digital cameras have both a viewfinder that you raise to your eye, and a monitor that's more like a TV. Most cameras with monitors allow instant picture review, so you can make sure you got the picture you wanted. If not, you can DELETE or ERASE the picture, and try again.

Most cameras with monitors also let you compose the image by watching the monitor, instead of bringing the tiny viewfinder to your eye. This can be a lot of fun, and makes shooting at crazy angles a lot easier. (See pages 46 and 47.) But be careful—monitors use up battery power quickly. Some cameras offer cool designs that let you twist and turn the monitor. This, too, is great for shooting at crazy angles.

Bigger is better when it comes to monitors! It makes it easier to PLAYBACK your pictures and ERASE them on the fly (see pages 30 and 31). A viewfinder that allows you to see exactly what the lens sees is ideal. An electronic viewfinder or a through-the-lens (TTL) viewfinder can do this. If your camera doesn't have one of these kinds of viewfinders, you may see a slightly different version of the scene when shooting close subjects.

REMOVABLE MEMORY

Another extremely important feature for a digital camera is where it saves the image. Most cameras record the image on a removable memory card or stick. This can be removed and put into a computer slot or a card reader when you are ready to transfer your pictures to the computer. Or you can connect the camera directly to the computer through a cord, dock, or wireless connection.

But you may not be able to carry around a computer with you, or you simply may not have the time to DOWNLOAD the pictures. In these cases, it's great to have a camera

with one of the many types of removable memory cards or memory sticks.

Like film, you load the card or stick into the camera, record your images onto it, remove it when it's full, and replace it with a blank one to begin shooting again.

When you're ready, place the full card into a card reader (or camera) that's hooked to the computer. Then SAVE the images to the computer, ERASE the card, and shoot new pictures on the same card.

When buying extra cards, make sure you pick the right type for your camera, such as Compact Flash or Smart Media.

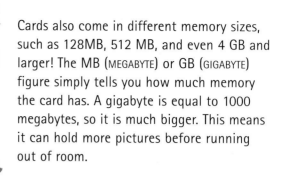

Cards also come in different memory sizes, such as 128MB, 512 MB, and even 4 GB and larger! The MB (MEGABYTE) or GB (GIGABYTE) figure simply tells you how much memory the card has. A gigabyte is equal to 1000 megabytes, so it is much bigger. This means it can hold more pictures before running out of room.

EXPOSURE MODES

The simplest cameras simply choose the "best" preprogrammed exposure, with results dependent

FEATURES	BENEFITS
1. Resolution	How many megapixels (millions of pixels) the camera can capture. Sometimes this is referred to as picture size.
2. Focus Capability	Make sure your camera autofocuses. Cheaper cameras call themselves focus-free or fixed-focus and they do NOT autofocus!
3. Removable Memory	This capability allows you switch the memory card/stick when it's full, so can keep shooting and don't have to rush to a computer to download.
4. Lens/Optical Zoom	A very important capability for designing your pictures. The wider the zoom range, the better. See pages 32 and 33 for details.
5. Digital Zoom	Digital zoom is not as good as optical zoom, because it just gets you closer by cropping the image and not optically zooming (see page 18).
6. Equivalent ISO	High "Equivalent ISO" ratings indicate that the camera has better low-light capability.
7. Flash Modes	You can achieve improved results if you camera offers specialty flash modes. See pages 36 to 40 for more details.
8. Exposure Modes	Specialty exposure modes can help you get better results with action, portrait, landscape, and close-up subjects.
9. Monitor	A monitor that allows you to playback pictures is a big benefit. Some also let you compose the image in the monitor (instead of the viewfinder).
10. Viewfinder	Some viewfinders just approximate what the camera sees, while others show you what the lens sees (called through-the-lens or ttl).

how well the camera's computers analyze the lighting. Some let you customize your exposures with EXPOSURE MODES for special situations.

EXPOSURE COMPENSATION

If you find that your pictures are too light or too dark, it could be that your camera is accidentally UNDEREXPOSING (too dark) or OVEREXPOSING (too light) the pictures in certain situations. +EV or –EV EXPOSURE COMPENSATION can correct this. Usually you'll need to use the +EV command for white or light subjects, and –EV for dark subjects.

FLASH MODES

Most cameras have a built-in flash, but they are not equal. Some digital cameras provide special FLASH MODES that can improve a lot of your pictures, and make really artsy results possible (see pages 36 to 40).

COLOR CONTROL

Color shooting modes are handy. Many cameras give you choices that include "normal" or neutral color, saturated color, black-and-white, or sepia (brownish "antique") images. If your camera don't offer these choices, you can make the same basic alterations in most photo-editing software programs.

FEATURES	BENEFITS
11. Self-Timer	You'll need a self-timer function if you want to do self-portraits! See page 29 for more details.
12. Macro Capability	Don't underestimate how much fun it is to take a close-up look at the world. Some cameras let you focus on subjects just inches away.
13. Color Modes	Color modes allow you to adjust the color of your pictures when you take them, including saturated color or "antique" (sepia) brown.
14. Movie Capability	Still pictures are great, but every once in a while it's nice to have movie/video capability. See page 41 for more information.
15. Power Supply	Digital cameras are power hogs, so check how many pictures it can take on one battery charge.
16. Accessories	A few cameras offer really cool accessories, like a special case (a housing) that lets you shoot picture pictures underwater!
17. Bundled Software	Many digital cameras come with a CD of bundled software. Look for photo-editing and printing software.
18. Connection Type	You need to match your camera (or a card reader) to one of the ports in your computer (such as usb or firewire), so you can transfer the pictures.
19. Size	Listen to Goldilocks! Some cameras are so big you won't want to carry them around. Others are so small that the controls are hard to use.
20. Price	Buy only what you need today, because by the time you need to upgrade to bigger and better, those "cutting edge" cameras will be affordable.

Scanning Prints, Film & Art

You may have older pictures taken with a film camera that you want to turn into digital photos. One of the quickest and least expensive ways to digitize your conventional photographs is to use a scanner and do it yourself. Low-priced models are available, and most offer PLUG-AND-PLAY simplicity. You simply attach the scanner to your computer via a cord, install the software, and you can get good results right out of the box.

There are four basic ways to scan:

1 PRINT (FLATBED) SCANNERS

Print or flatbed scanners look like the top portion of a photocopier machine. You lift the lid, place your print face down on the glass, and click on the SCAN command. Usually a scan window opens on your computer and "walks" you through the process. Most provide controls for CROPPING and SIZING. Some also let you adjust COLOR and CONTRAST. The scan takes a few seconds (or a few minutes for slow scanners or high-resolution images) before the image pops up on your computer. When it does, SAVE it, and you have a digital version of your photo!

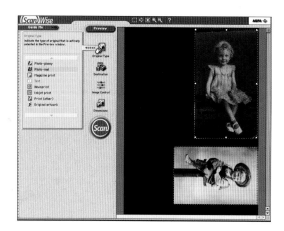

BOTTOM IMAGES: *Most scanners come with software that opens a CONTROL PANEL or WINDOW to walk you through the process (bottom left). This makes it easy to scan old prints from the family album (bottom right).*

Flatbed scanners can be used for more than just prints. You can scan your drawings, report cards, or any relatively flat object.

If you're careful not to scratch the glass, you can also scan 3D objects, such as fresh flowers, jewelry, stuffed animals, or merit badges (see page 24). Try draping a dark cloth over the items to produce a dark background. Black velvet is the best because it absorbs light and will scan darker.

If your objects are hard, moist, or have sharp edges, first lay a piece of clear acetate (such as blank overhead transparencies) on the glass to form a protective layer, then position your objects.

3 ALL-IN-ONE SCANNERS

Some scanners can scan prints, artwork, *and* film. Many also function as a photocopy machine and a printer.

4 STORES & LABS

If you don't want the bother of scanning older prints and negatives yourself, or you only have a few images to scan, you can consider having them done by a store or lab. *Watch out*—it may wipe out your savings, because it's not cheap. But it is easy. You simply bring in a stack of prints, negatives, or slides, then pay your money. You'll get back a CD with digitized versions of the pictures.

ABOVE: Flatbed scanners are great for scanning prints, artwork, and relatively flat objects.

RIGHT: Film scanners can scan film negatives and slides.

2 FILM SCANNERS

Transparency or film scanners are designed to shine light through a film to copy slides and negatives during the scanning process. Often they have film holders of different sizes to accommodate strips of negatives.

This Doesn't Look Like a Camera!

WHAT CAN YOU "SHOOT" WITH YOUR SCANNER?

Anything that is relatively flat works great, like a drawing, a Girl or Boy Scouts patch, and jewelry. But you can also shoot anything that can be smushed onto the glass, like a teddy bear, your soccer uniform, or a quilting project.

If the objects are too thick and you can't close the cover, drape a piece of fabric over the top. Dark fabrics work best. A tablecloth or large shirt will do the trick. Black velvet is the very best if you want a rich background color.

CAREFUL!

Be really careful not to scratch the glass on the scanner! It's a good idea to put some thick clear plastic between hard objects and the glass. (Ask your parents if they have acetate or overhead transparency materials.) In a pinch, you can tape plastic from see-through bag or plastic wrap down on the glass.

ABOVE: *Placing a box or cloth over the scanner makes the true colors come out.*

LEFT: *With the lid open and no covering, the feathers appear translucent. Which version is "best" is a matter of opinion.*

SLOPPY STUFF

You can even scan sloppy wet stuff if you put it in a very clear plastic container (like the kind berries come in). We scanned alphabet pasta and sauce. Drape cloth or an upside-down box over the container to make a dark background.

WARNING! NOTHING LIVE!

Don't be tempted to put your pet on the glass, or press your face down. The bright light is really bad for anything living.

Learn Your Camera

There are a few camera controls you'll want to learn how to use quickly and confidently. Focus Lock, Zooming, Flash, and Exposure modes will give you a lot of creative options. And it only takes a few minutes of practice to master them.

Get Focused!

Your camera might be an autofocus camera, but that doesn't mean it focuses well every time! It's kind of a stupid machine that sometimes needs your brain power to deliver great results.

Most digital cameras only know how to focus on what is in the exact center of the viewfinder. That's great, until your subject is off center.

The photo on the top of the next page is a typical portrait you might take of two friends. *But what's in the dead center of the picture?* Far away trees (as shown in the red circle). So the camera focuses on the distant trees. And if the trees are far enough away from your subjects, the people could be out of focus and look blurry in the photo.

To prevent this, you'll need to activate FOCUS LOCK. Simply center the camera on one of the subjects (such as the red circle in the center pictures), and push the shutter halfway down. When you do this, the picture won't be framed right, but don't worry. You're just telling the camera where you want it to focus. Next, without lifting your finger, swing the camera back to where you want it, and press the shutter the rest of the way down.

Check the picture in PLAYBACK mode to make sure you got it right. If you do it five or 10 times, it will become second nature and you'll soon be using FOCUS LOCK almost without thinking about it.

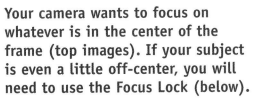Your camera wants to focus on whatever is in the center of the frame (top images). If your subject is even a little off-center, you will need to use the Focus Lock (below).

FOCUS LOCK is also helpful when shooting sports if you find your camera is too slow at autofocusing on a moving subject. Instead, you can guess where the action will be (such as home base, or the finish line in a race). Then use FOCUS LOCK to pre-focus on the right spot by pushing and holding the shutter button halfway down. When the action arrives, just push the shutter the rest of the way down, and you'll get a perfectly focused, perfectly timed picture. See page 58 for more on action shots.

Sharp Pictures

Bad focus is one way to get blurry pictures. Another is if your camera is selecting too slow a shutter speed. *What's a shutter speed?* That's the amount of time the camera needs to open up a hole (or window) in the

LEFT: *You know where home plate is! As the runner starts for the base, pre-focus on the spot using FOCUS LOCK, and then take the picture as the action happens. You can also try panning the camera (see page 58).*

lens so that light can shine through and record the scene on the camera's imaging device. A certain amount of light is needed for a proper exposure. In dim lighting, the camera must leave this hole open for a longer period of time to record the image.

Image blurring occurs if the hole is open long enough for the subject or camera to move *while* the image is being recorded.

FOUR LEFT IMAGES: *In dim lighting, a picture can turn out blurry because while the picture was being taken either the camera shook, the subject moved, or both. It's not as obvious in the full version (far top left), but when it's blown up large (near top left) it looks bad.*

Solutions for a sharper picture (far bottom left) include switching to a HIGHER EQUIVALENT ISO, steadying the camera (see page 29), and asking your subject to "hold still." Even when blown up large (near bottom left) it still looks sharp.

You'll rarely get blurred images on a bright sunny day, because your camera can select fast shutter speeds that "freeze" motion. But as the light gets dimmer, there's more chance that you'll accidentally get blur.

Three things can fix this:

1 MOVE INTO A BRIGHTER AREA

Improve the lighting by opening up window blinds, turning on the room lights, or moving outdoors.

2 TURN ON THE FLASH

Add light by turning on our camera's built-in flash. (See pages 36 to 40.)

3 A HIGHER EQUIVALENT ISO

Select a higher number EQUIVALENT ISO if it is available on your camera.

Equivalent ISO

Some cameras offer an EQUIVALENT ISO setting. This is similar to the ISO ratings of film, and indicates their low-light capability (with a higher number being better). On some cameras it can be set to AUTOMATIC, 100, 200, 400, and sometimes higher.

If you're shooting in low light and your shots are blurry, switch to a higher number setting. This will help you get sharper images, but it will reduce the overall quality, so when you move back into brighter light, remember to put it back to the lower number or to AUTO.

Get in the Picture!

Sometimes it's no fun being the one taking the pictures because you're not in them. Well, most cameras offer a SELF-TIMER, usually indicated by a symbol of a clock or stopwatch. When you activate the SELF-TIMER and then press the shutter button, the SELF-TIMER will delay the picture-taking for 10 or 15 seconds. If you're clever, you can place the camera on a solid object such as a table, hit the SELF-TIMER, and then run around to get in front of the lens, so you're in the picture too.

The best way to steady your camera is with a tripod. They come in big, expensive models, as well as in inexpensive pocket sizes. With a pocket tripod, you simple open the legs, screw on the camera (there should be a screw thread on the bottom), place it on a steady table or other object of the right height, and shoot.

You can also come up with novel solutions, such as nestling your camera in a coat or on top of a bag of rice.

Warning! Some cameras will focus on the scene when you first activate the SELF-TIMER, so it could misfocus on the background instead of you and your friends (see pages 26 and 27). If you find this happening, pick a spot that's against a wall, or have your friends stand in the center of the frame, and then try again.

Why Use Playback?

Most digital cameras will let you review your pictures in PLAYBACK mode after you take them. You can scroll through the pictures in the memory one at a time. Often you can view four, nine, or 16 images at a time if you want to locate a particular picture quickly.

A nice feature is the ability to MAGNIFY each image by pushing a symbol of a magnifying glass with a + (magnify) or - (shrink) marking. You can use it to see the details of the picture, such as if your subject has a good expression or if the subject is in focus.

CONSERVING BATTERIES

The only reason to turn off the monitor is if you're worried about battery power. One of the quickest ways to run down the batteries is to view the scene with the monitor, and play it back to watch afterwards. If you're worried about stretching your battery power, use the viewfinder to shoot pictures, and wait to view the pictures.

Also check the menu settings to see if the post-picture "review" (usually two seconds) can be turned off. You'll find you can take a lot more pictures before having to change or recharge the batteries.

Trash It!

Don't be afraid to DELETE or ERASE pictures that aren't very good. They fill up the memory, and you'll waste time transferring them into the computer. This includes out of focus images or pictures that don't look good. The MAGNIFY button (see above) will help you check the details.

The ERASE control (sometimes called DELETE or TRASH) is usually indicated by a symbol of a garbage can. Be careful to read the MENU when you use the ERASE feature, because you can erase a single picture or *all* the pictures in the memory.

BELOW: *most cameras allow you to* PLAYBACK *your photos after you take them. Some let you view multiple pictures at a time to quickly locate an image (left), full frame (center) or magnified (right).*

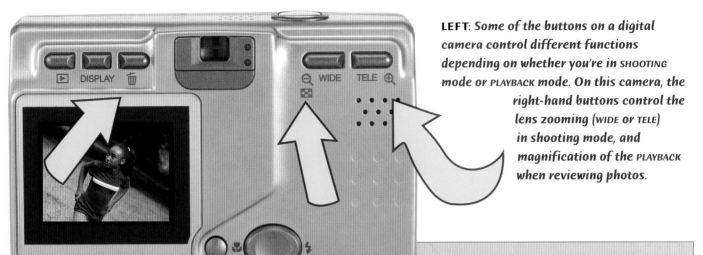

LEFT: *Some of the buttons on a digital camera control different functions depending on whether you're in* SHOOTING *mode or* PLAYBACK *mode. On this camera, the right-hand buttons control the lens zooming (*WIDE *or* TELE*) in shooting mode, and magnification of the* PLAYBACK *when reviewing photos.*

ABOVE: *The symbol of a garbage can allows you to* ERASE *images you have already shot.*

RIGHT: *Being able to review your pictures moments after you take them is one of the best features of a digital camera.*

Cameras with Zoom

Zoom lenses are a great feature, because without moving your feet you can dramatically change what's included in the picture. By zooming to the TELE or T setting, you can "get closer" to your subject. At the WIDE or W setting, you can include more of the scene in front of you, which is really helpful when you're trying to fit a bunch of people into the image.

OPTICAL OR DIGITAL?

The best kind of zoom is OPTICAL ZOOM. Optical means that the lens changes so that the image is magnified as you go from wide to tele. This delivers much higher quality images than DIGITAL ZOOM, which magnifies the image by cropping (see page 62) and enlarging the center portion. This in effect reduces the resolution and therefore the quality.

The only benefit of DIGITAL ZOOM is that it saves time later because you won't have to crop the image in photo-editing software to make it look bigger. In general, turn off the DIGITAL ZOOM, and just use the OPTICAL ZOOM if available. Walk closer to the subject if you want it bigger.

Wide

Tele

THIS PAGE:

Zooming isn't just for making your subjects bigger. It can also change how they look. In the above images, the photographer moved to keep the girls the same size in both the wide and tele modes. Look below to compare how the background (and the tree) changed.

Background Check

Your zoom lens setting can have a huge affect on the final look of your photograph. A WIDE lens setting was chosen for the first picture (above left), then the TELE setting (above right). In the WIDE version, the photographer was just a few feet away from the subjects, and the two girls fill the frame.

When the photographer switched to the TELE zoom setting, at that same distance the photo would only have showed their heads. So the photographer stepped back until the two girls fit into the photograph (from head to toe) and took the picture.

Notice the difference in how the girls look. The TELE setting is probably the most flattering. But the biggest difference is the background. The girls didn't move an inch, yet the trees in the TELE version now looks huge, and you can't see any sky.

Pretty cool, huh? Try experimenting by moving closer and farther away from your subject, while zooming the camera to keep them about the same size in the picture. For more information on backgrounds, see pages 53 to 57.

Background looks small

Background looks huge

Making Funny Faces...

Both lens settings & software create fun distortions.

The TELE or T setting on your zoom camera is the BEST choice for portraits if you want the person to look his or her best (see page 43). However, if you want to get a little crazy and create some distortions, read on!

THIS PAGE: *Shooting from a distance with the TELE lens setting may make you look the best (above), but getting close and WIDE sure is perfect if you're determined to goof it up for the camera.*

WIDE-ANGLE LENS SETTING

For the most dramatic lens effects, set the camera to the WIDE or W lens setting, and move close to your subject.

You'll need to learn your camera's minimal focusing distance to make sure your results are sharp. Some cameras will beep or shine a light in the viewfinder if you are too close. Others will refuse to shoot. You can always read the instruction manual to find out how close you can get.

Or just try it, and then check the monitor playback. Use the MAGNIFICATION option to blow up the picture on the monitor so you can really check the focus. (If your camera has this option, it will usually be activated by the button with a magnifying glass with the symbols "+" or "–" inside.)

SOFTWARE DISTORTIONS

Some photo-editing and specialty software (like Kai's SuperGoo) let you quickly create silly distortions of your photographs—like bug eyes and pinched faces (above).

For the most dramatic effects, start with lens distortion (far left) and then add software distortions (below). See chapter 4 for more awesome things you can do with software.

News Flash!

When you're indoors or the lighting is dim, your camera may not be able to take sharp pictures because there's not enough light. The result is a big blur.

However, some cameras will automatically add flash, so you have enough light to get an unblurry picture. On other cameras, you may have to manually push a button or pop up the flash.

REALITY CHECK

The small, built-in flash on most point-and-shoot cameras is not very powerful. It's important to understand the limitations of this flash in terms of the range of distances where it works well. If you're too close (a few feet), then the subject may be too brightly lit because the camera can't reduce the flash's power enough.

If you're too far away, then it can't reach far enough and the subject will be dark. A good example of this would be an evening baseball game. The camera wants to light up the distant ball players, but you'd need huge stadium lights to do that! Check the instruction manual for the flash range on your camera.

Flash requires a lot of battery power, and it can sometimes take a few seconds for the flash to recharge. Depending on the camera, the camera may refuse to shoot again until the flash is ready, or it may take the picture anyway at less than full power (probably resulting in a subject that's too dark). Check your instruction manual so you'll know when it's safe to shoot again.

If your batteries are getting weak, the camera may still be able to take pictures but not have enough strength to fully power the flash. This could happen even if the "low battery" symbol might not yet be showing.

FLASH MODES

Some digital cameras have special FLASH MODES that let you get better pictures or create crazy effects.

1 AUTOFLASH

This is the camera's automatic flash mode. If the camera thinks the lighting is too dark, it will automatically fire the flash. Sometimes this might not be what you want, in which case you can select FLASH OFF (see page 38).

2 RED-EYE REDUCTION FLASH

Red-eye is that annoying "devilish" red color that fills the eyes of some people in flash pictures.

RED-EYE REDUCTION FLASH mode causes a bright lamp or series of flashes to go off before you actually take pictures, reducing this effect.

Unfortunately, this can be annoying and causes a delay before the picture is taken. Your subjects may not have red-eye, but they could have a startled look or may have already looked away because they thought the pre-flash was the picture moment.

Instead, you can risk producing the red-eye effect, and then improve it on the computer later. Easy RED-EYE repair functions are found in some photo-editing software, such as Microsoft Picture It or MGI PhotoSuite.

BELOW: *Red-eye sometimes occurs when photographing people in dim lighting. It can be reduced or eliminated using* RED-EYE REDUCTION FLASH *mode or in photo-editing software on the computer.*

It's not Halloween! So why did she get those red demon eyes?

3 FILL-FLASH

FILL FLASH is the quickest way to make significant improvements in many of your outdoor pictures. In bright, sunny situations, the sun can cause deep shadows on the faces of your subjects that hide their features.

The AUTOFLASH feature on most cameras fires when the lighting gets dim. FILL FLASH, on the other hand, forces the flash to fire even in these bright situations. The flash then fills the shadow without having a major effect on the main light (the sun).

It also adds attractive highlights to your subject's eyes. Because this feature makes such a significant improvement in your pictures, when in doubt, use it!

4 NIGHT (OR SLOW) FLASH

Occasionally, you'll want to take a backlit or nighttime portrait with an interesting background, such as city lights or the last glimmer of a sunset.

If your camera has NIGHT FLASH mode (sometimes called SLOW SYNC flash), this is a good time to use it. NIGHT FLASH mode combines a flash exposure (which illuminates a nearby subject) with a longer shutter speed (see page 28) to get a good picture.

For optimal results, steady the camera with a tripod or brace it against a solid object to keep the background sharp.

5 FLASH OFF

Most cameras will automatically fire the flash if the light is dim (AUTOFLASH mode). Sometimes natural lighting can be wonderful by itself, such as at dawn or dusk. If this is the case, you may want to overrule the camera's setting and turn the flash off. Usually this mode is indicated by a symbol of a lighting bolt symbol and the "no" circle-and-slash symbol around it.

If you choose FLASH OFF in low-light or dimmer lighting situations, your camera will be using a relatively slow shutter speed.

(Continued on page 40.)

LEFT: *Turn the flash off for candles, jack o'lanterns, fireworks, and neon signs.*

Nasty Shadows Ruining Your Pictures?

In bright sunlight, your camera doesn't "think" it needs to add light by firing the flash. However, sunlight can cause dark shadows on the faces of your subjects, especially if they're wearing hats with visors or brims.

But you're smarter than the camera! When you see dark shadows on the faces of your subjects, turn on the FILL-FLASH feature. This will lighten the shadows, without affecting other parts of the picture very much. The higher the sun is in the sky, the longer and darker the shadows will be. So high noon is the perfect time for FILL-FLASH.

This can cause the picture to be blurred unless you steady the camera (see pages 28 and 29).

You can do this by using a tripod, bracing it on a steady object, or snuggling it in a coat or towel. Switching to a higher EQUIVALENT ISO on your digital camera will also help you get sharper results (see page 29).

FLASH OFF can also be used for candles, such as a birthday cake or a jack o'lantern. A candle can sometimes produce enough light for a cool-looking picture. Set the camera to FLASH OFF or you'll ruin the effect by over-powering the candle's light with the flash (see the examples below).

Flash On vs. Flash Off

Trying Flash Off? Hold the camera very steady or you'll end up with a blur.

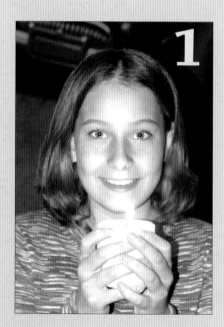

The camera fires the flash (AUTOFLASH mode) because the lighting is dim.

FLASH OFF mode, but the camera or subject moved causing blurring.

FLASH OFF mode, but this time the camera is held steady and the subject stayed still.

Exposure Modes

Some high-end cameras offer special EXPO-SURE MODES that help the camera perform in certain situations.

The most common EXPOSURE MODE is the PROGRAM (P) or AUTOMATIC mode. This is the fully automated mode of the camera. It will set the camera controls for the average subject, making it a good choice for every-day snapshots. Some cameras only offer this mode.

PORTRAIT exposure mode is, not surprisingly, a great choice for portraits. This mode tells the camera to try to throw the background out of focus so the emphasis is on your subject.

An out-of-focus background tends to be most attractive in portraiture because it eliminates distractions in the background that would take away from the impact of the main subject. Your camera CONTROL DIAL or LCD PANEL may have a symbol of a head-and-shoulders to indicate this mode.

ACTION mode sets the camera so that the shutter speed is as fast as possible. This will result in the sharpest (least blurred) result.

BELOW: Some cameras offer an ACTION mode for shooting fast-moving subjects.

BOTTOM RIGHT: Many digital cameras have close-focusing capability. Some even offer a CLOSE-UP or MACRO mode.

MACRO or CLOSE-UP mode, usually depicted by a flower symbol, optimizes the camera for shooting small subjects up close.

Movie Mode

Many cameras have a MOVIE mode that takes short movies that you can play back on the computer. On better cameras, the movies look quite smooth and the sound quality is great. Some cameras offer several movie choices, including a low-resolution version for smaller file sizes (better for emailing), and a fast frame rate for movies of fast-moving subjects.

Take Great Pictures

Once you know how to operate your camera, you can start taking snapshots. However, if you want to move from "just plain snapshots" to really great pictures, you'll want to check out some of these easy techniques.

The term COMPOSITION is a word that's often used to describe how a picture or painting is designed. You may instinctively know that one picture looks better than many of your other snapshots, but it might not be easy to figure out exactly why. Most of the photos you really like probably have good COMPOSITIONS. Pinpointing what makes a composition good or bad can be a challenge.

The tips and techniques shown in this chapter should help you figure this out by helping you design better photographs (and therefore create better compositions). Once you know why certain techniques improve your pictures, then they can all be winners.

The WIDE ANGLE *version (above) makes the curly haired girl's face look wide and almost comical. The version below (shot farther away with the* TELE *setting) is more flattering.*

The combination of a WIDE *lens setting, and a close shooting distance makes the girl on the left look younger than she really is by distorting her face. Because younger kids tend to have larger, chubbier faces (compared to their bodies), the lens distortion makes this girl look younger than she is!*

In the version to the right, she looks closer to how she looks in person. It was shot from farther away with the lens zoomed to the TELE *setting.*

Zoooooom to Tele for Portraits

When you shoot portraits with a WIDE zoom lens setting, the picture gets distorted. You might not realize it, but the photo will somehow seem less pleasing and your subject may even look "fat." The closer you get to the subject and the closer to WIDE the lens setting, the weirder it looks.

For a flattering portrait, step back and zoom all the way out to the TELE or T setting. Then step back until you have the composition you want. Usually for portraits, this means a head-and-shoulders picture. If space is limited, do the best you can.

SEEING EYE TO EYE

My favorite portraiture trick is simple. Determine your subject's eye level and raise or lower yourself to the same level.

Most people shoot at their own standing eye level and rarely change to different levels. This is fine and dandy if every friend and family member you have is your *exact* height. But what about shorter siblings? You'll be looking down on them. Or taller parents? You'll be looking up at them. And how about people sitting on chairs, lying on the floor, or hanging from the monkey bars?

Try to match their height to take the picture, even if it means getting down on your knees or stepping up on a stool. It may sound like a lot of extra effort, but you'll be amazed in the difference it can make in your portraits.

The chart below will help get you started, But the basic rule is to think about your height *before* you shoot. It may sound simple, but it really works. Then check out pages 46 and 47 for exceptions to the rule!

Subject Type		Shooting Position
	Same Height Friend	Shoot from your normal standing position.
	People Who Are Taller than You	Stand on a chair, a step, or even your tip-toes.
	Standing Toddler	You're taller than a two-year-old, so get on your knees or squat low.
	Sitting Person or Pet on Chair	Sit on a chair across from the subject, or squat to a sitting height.
	Person or Pet Lying on the Ground	Get down on the ground, so you'll be at their eye level.
	Unusual Angle	*Look up! Look Down!* Position yourself or your subject high or low, such as on a balcony, cliff, or edge of a pool.

Lying on the ground and looking up at the photographer is not a very comfortable position. It also creates an odd and confusing angle.

Compare this to when the photographer also lies down on the floor. Not only is the photograph more flattering, but it's more friendly.

Break the Rules!

It's easy to get stuck in a rut—go high & low for crazy angles.

PLAY THE ANGLES!

Most snapshots are taken from the photographer's eye level while standing. As described on pages 44 and 45, this is not usually the best angle for portraits of people who are lower or higher than your eye level. Many of these pictures can be improved by changing that shooting angle.

Since we spend our lives seeing the world from our own eye level, standing shots are the most common angle of view. You can really shake things up by getting down low or up high to shoot a picture.

Try lying on the ground or shooting down from a stairwell. And when everyone else is looking straight ahead, try looking up or down.

You can exaggerate your new perspective by coming in close with a wide-angle lens or zooming in from far away.

Gotcha!

Portraits of your friends smiling at the camera are fine, but after a while they can get kind of boring. Some of the most successful photos of people are taken when the subject isn't paying attention to your camera.

CARRY YOUR CAMERA

Start by remembering to carry your camera with you on a regular basis. You just never know when your friends are going to start doing something fun or interesting. When they do, just casually take out your camera and take the photo without making a fuss.

ZOOM TO TELE

If your camera has a zoom lens, you can zoom to the TELE or T setting. This will allow you to shoot frame-filling pictures from a

LEFT: *Stealth and using the monitor to shoot from the hip will help you get great candid pictures of your friends doing cool stuff.*

LEFT: *Exploring is a great time to carry your camera!*

RIGHT: *Digital pictures are free, so take a lot. You can erase all the bad ones—you just need one good one!*

distance. The further away from your subject you can get, the less likely they will notice what you're doing.

USE THE MONITOR

Some digital cameras have the advantage of a monitor that lets you compose the picture without having to bring the camera to your eye. Not only is this convenient, but you can be very sneaky about your photography— *regular spy stuff!* The more you practice, the better you'll get at "shooting from the hip" to get great unposed (candid) pictures.

BRATTY BROTHER SYNDROME

Mastering the monitor will also come in handy if your little brother keeps being a

goof in shot after shot after shot. Don't give up. Just make him think you're not ready to take the picture, by moving the camera further away from your eye and face. Then just take quick peeks to make sure you're pointed in the right direction. When he *finally* acts normal, you can click off the picture! Luckily it's digital, so you can DELETE, DELETE, DELETE the bad versions.

This works great for pets too. If you have a dog, you've probably noticed that every time you point the camera in his direction, he comes running over because he thinks you're looking at him. But if you hold the camera low and look down at the monitor, you'll have a lot less trouble.

Everyone Say, "Cheese!"

Photographing a group of people is actually a difficult thing to do well. For starters, just shooting everyone smiling and with their eyes open can be tough. Here are some hints:

1 TAKE A LOT OF PICTURES

The only insurance is to take a lot of pictures and hope that everyone's eyes are open and hope for the best. If you take five or six shots, you have a much better chance.

2 AVOID THE LINE-UP SHOT

Beyond taking a zillion pictures, the next trick is to get creative with the posing. Usually, your first instinct will be to line up everyone with their shoulders next to each other for the picture. This is rarely the best composition, and you end up with a picture that looks like a police line-up.

3 SOME IN FRONT, SOME BEHIND

Instead, just try to put the heads at different heights. This makes the composition more exciting. It also has the added bonus of

BELOW: *Compare the line-up pictures on the bottom left, with the version where every one is on a picnic bench and their heads are at different levels. Not only do these look better, but you can see their faces better because they are larger (compare the yellow oval sizes).*

tightening the group so you can move or zoom in closer to make the faces larger.

The simplest way is the "sports team" photo pose. To do this is to make several rows, with the front line sitting, kneeling, or even lying down. Seat your parents (or an especially tall or short person) so they don't stick out from the group.

4 THE STACKING OR STAIR METHOD

Instead of rows, you can use a staircase, picnic bench, or boulder to put people at different heights so everyone's face is fully visible in the picture.

5 SOFTWARE COMBINATIONS

Perhaps the most entertaining method is to shoot separate images of different people and combine them into one picture using STITCHING or COLLAGING software. See pages 70 and 71 for more details.

RIGHT IMAGES: *Try to "stack" your subjects so their heads are at different levels and they're grouped more closely. Not only does this look better, but it lets you make them bigger in the final photo (previous page and far right images). Or it gives you the room to show a dramatic background, like Delicate Arch in Arches National Park (near right).*

Off-Centered

When designing your pictures, your first instinct will probably be to center your subject in the center of the viewfinder like a bull's eye target. However, this is rarely the best photograph.

A handy guideline is to put the main subject off to the side, instead of in the dead center of the frame. It's sometimes called the RULE OF THIRDS because the best place to position the subject is along the outer third of the photo.

To understand the RULE OF THIRDS, draw an imaginary tic-tac-toe board over the picture (bottom left image), and place the subject along one of the lines. Notice how the boy and girl are along the left line, and the boy's face is on the intersection point.

In the comparison shown at the bottom right, the straight portrait has the boy's face smack in the center. But by moving him off to the side, the picture has a stronger design.

Experienced photographers often take it to further extremes, placing subjects even farther away from the center of the frame than the guideline of one-third.

This doesn't mean your main subject always has to be off center, but quite often, it is the best choice. This is especially true if the background helps to tell the story of the picture (see pages 56 and 57).

When shooting an off-center composition, be sure to use the FOCUS LOCK function, or your your subject may be out of focus. See pages 26 and 27 for details.

RIGHT: *Moving your main subject off to one side often improves the picture.*

LEFT: *The yellow lines in the far bottom left picture demonstrate how the subjects are placed along one of the lines that divides the picture into thirds.*

Creating Better Backgrounds

THIS PAGE: *Okay, okay, the "photo" below is a joke. But it serves to show how colors, words, and clutter can rob the attention from your main subject! Compare this to the photo on the right.*

One of the quickest ways to wreck a good picture is to have a bad background. You may be so excited about the subject in front of you that you completely ignore what's behind.

The main subject is great, so who cares about the background? Unfortunately, when you enlarge your pictures, you'll care. Suddenly the picture doesn't look half as good as it did

in the viewfinder or on the monitor. *Why?* Because when you were taking the picture, you had "tunnel vision." All you saw was the subject at the end of the tunnel, and not everything else around it. But later, when you or your friends look at the picture, this other non-subject stuff will look terrible. Whoever is looking at the picture will be distracted by unimportant elements in the picture.

REMOVE THE CLUTTER
You clean up your room *(sometimes)*, so why not "clean up" your photos too? Try to minimize background clutter and avoid distracting elements (see page 57).

WATCH FOR ANTLERS
Poles, trees and other vertical objects in the background may look like they're "growing" out of your subject's head like the antlers of a deer. Just a step to the right or left can often shift them in relation to your subject.

AVOID BRIGHT HIGHLIGHTS

Bright areas in the background tend to draw the viewer's attention away from the subject. Watch out for reflection off metal and bright lights.

GOOD COLORS, WRONG PLACE

Bold colors (like red or yellow) can also be distracting if they appear as spots in the background.

LEAVE OUT YOUR ABC'S

Words and text, such as signs and billboards almost *beg* to be read. If they say something important to the story of the picture (see pages 56 and 57), you can leave them in. But if not, you're better off getting rid of them.

What would be a sign you might leave in a picture? Leave in the "Dr. Smith's Dentistry" sign when you take a picture of your sister with her nice straight teeth on the day her braces come off!

CROOKED CAMERA

A picture that was taken with the camera held crookedly will cause the background to look as if it's sliding to one side or the other, as if you were on a sinking ship. Luckily this is easy to fix in the computer by rotating the image to straighten the background (see pages 60 and 61).

Improve Your Backgrounds

Now you know what makes a background bad, but what's the cure? Take the picture, and then very carefully look for the following previously mentioned background problems that can spoil an otherwise good potential picture.

The picture shown of puppies sitting on somebody's lap (far left picture) is an example of a bad background choice. The cut-off head makes you want to ask, *"Who is that person?"* Plus, the colorful T-shirt design makes the background very distracting.

You can avoid many of the background problems by performing one or more of these actions:

1 Move the subjects so they are positioned against a less cluttered background. Here, the tired pups were placed on the floor and then repositioned when they were soundly asleep.

2 Zoom in with the TELE setting (or step closer) to fill more of the frame with the subject, thereby eliminating more of the background distractions (the bottom of the couch and chair in this case).

3 Move to the left, right, up or down to change your angle, so the background changes in relation to the subject.

4 Use photo-editing software to retouch a cluttered background or remove a distracting object. You can also use photo-editing software to crop the image so that the subject is more prominent and the background is no longer part of the image (see page 61).

Tell a Story

The old proverb states: "A picture is worth a thousand words." *But not every picture!* It's up to you, the photographer, to decide what story to tell with each photograph, and how many words it will be worth.

Many of the tips in this book have emphasized filling the frame with the all-important subject. However, sometimes it's better to include more of the background. A portrait is a portrait after all. But a picture can also tell the story of an event, such as cutting down the perfect Christmas tree.

If the background helps tell the story of the photograph, such as this family trip to an ancient ruin (right), include it so the person viewing your picture will get a good look at the surroundings.

Zoom the camera lens to the WIDE setting to get as much of the scene in the picture as possible. If you camera doesn't have a zoom, step back as far as you can.

Placing the people off-center is also a good idea, because it usually produces a better COMPOSITION. (See page 52 for more details on off-centered pictures.) If your subjects aren't in the middle, be sure to use FOCUS LOCK before shooting the picture. (See pages 26 and 27 for information on FOCUS LOCK.)

THIS PAGE: *The background in the top and bottom photos are important parts of these pictures, because they tell us about a trip to a ruin (top) or that the boy has just chopped down this Christmas tree (left). The middle shot of just the brother and sister is a simple portrait, but reveals almost nothing about where they are.*

A big maroon chair and the
radiator in the background
attract our eye.

A pile of books
adds no important
information
to the picture,
but instead
makes the
room looked more
cluttered, and the
picture confusing.

Careful! Not *Too* Much Background!

Often there will be *too* much stuff in the background for a good picture, and you'll need to simplify it. Determine which elements are important to your picture and eliminate the rest.

The image above contains a lot of distracting items that don't tell the story of this Christmas chess showdown. The arrows point to a cluttered bookcase, a maroon chair, and a bright red plastic cup.

To create a better background, the photographer chose a different shooting angle for the photo on the left. At first glance, the Christmas tree in the background could be considered distracting, because of the bright colored lights. However, it's an important part of the picture because it tells us that it's Christmas.

Catch the Action

For the best looking pictures of a moving subject (especially one that's moving from left to right, or right to left), you should PAN your camera. Basically, this means you follow the subject in the viewfinder before, during, and after you take the photograph.

In general, this will result in the sharpest action pictures. When the light is too dim for sharp photos of fast-moving subjects, the panning technique will help you get artistically blurred pictures.

To pan, stand with your feet slightly apart and both hands holding the camera. Then, twist your upper body and hips without moving your feet, while keeping the subject centered in the viewfinder or monitor. Try not to bob up and down, and keep the motion as smooth as possible.

If you find you're missing the peak of the action, it may be because your camera is slow to focus. If this is the case, push the shutter slightly before the perfect moment. Or use FOCUS LOCK (see pages 26 and 27) to pre-focus on the spot your subject will pass.

Perfect panning pictures take practice. Stand on the sidewalk and practice on passing cars or bicycles. Once you've mastered panning, you'll be amazed at how great your action shots look.

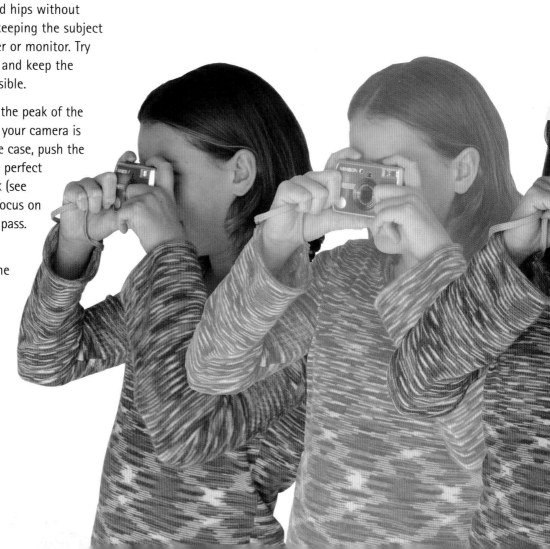

FAR LEFT: *This action photo is sharp because the photographer used the panning technique described on the previous page. Even on bright days, you may need to pan to get sharp images of fast subjects.*

NEAR LEFT: *Dim light prevented a sharp image of this running dog. However, panning saved the day by making it an artistic image.*

Notice how the dog is relatively sharp, when compared to the background. This is because the panning kept the dog sort of still (centered) in the viewfinder during the long exposure, while the background changed (and thus blurred). Legs go back and forth and heads bob more than the torso of the dog, so these are more blurred.

BOTTOM: *Proper panning requires that you track the subject in the viewfinder as it moves across the scene in front of you. Keep your feet planted and swing your hips in a smooth motion while keeping the subject in the center of the viewfinder.*

Software Magic

Once you download your pictures to your computer, the fun begins! You can improve them, change them, combine them, and more.

Improve Your Images with Software

Today's PICTURE-EDITING SOFTWARE makes it easy to improve your pictures. Many computers, digital cameras, and printers come with simple software. You can also buy many excellent programs. Top choices include: Adobe Photoshop Elements, MGI PhotoSuite, Microsoft Picture It, Scansoft PhotoFactory, and Ulead PhotoImpact.

You can alter digital pictures in several basic ways by using controls such as CROPPING, ROTATING, DODGING/BURNING, and altering COLOR MODES, CONTRAST, and BRIGHTNESS.

You can also change your images by adding artistic blurs, combining photos, morphing and "goo-ing," and distortions of all types.

Rotate Your Images

You may need to rotate your picture if it shows up on your computer sideways or upside-down.

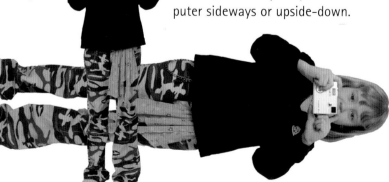

The ROTATE (or similarly named) command can usually be done in quarter turns (90°) CLOCKWISE or COUNTER-CLOCKWISE, as well as half turns (180°). Select ARBITRARY ROTATION to straighten an image if you accidentally shot it slightly crooked. You can also FLIP the picture to reverse it.

Crop It!

One of the quickest ways to improve your photograph is to crop out unimportant parts of the picture. You'll be amazed how quickly trimming off the edges can improve the image by drawing attention to the main subject (see pages 53 to 55).

You can use cropping to get a "closer look" at a portion of a picture, such as the eye in this tree frog picture. Tree frogs are skittish fellows, so even if the camera was capable of getting that close, the photographer wouldn't have been able to do so without scaring it off.

If you shoot at the camera's highest RESOLUTION (see pages 9 to 12), even after you CROP the image, you'll probably have enough pix-

els left to print a nice picture of just the eye. If you save the original and the cropped versions under different names, you're getting two-for-one out of your pictures! This was the case in the school term paper shown below.

You can also use cropping to eliminate bad or boring backgrounds (see pages 54 and 55) or to turn a horizontal picture into a vertical.

Tree Frogs

**Science Report
by Manuel Rodriguez**

**Field Trip
to the Zoo
February 18**

Tree frogs have bright orange eyes. They bulge out and move quickly.

When they sleep they have a protective eye cover that looks like a lace window shade. You can still see their eyes behind it.

Red-Eye Correction

Everyone has seen photographs where the subject's eyes appear a demonic red. The RED-EYE REDUCTION FLASH mode on some cameras will reduce it by firing a pre-flash or shining a bright lamp before taking the picture. Many people find this light and the delay it causes annoying (see pages 36 and 37).

Instead, many photo-editing programs, such as PhotoSuite and Picture It, have simple RED-EYE functions that enable you to click on the eyes in the picture to quickly and automatically neutralize the red coloring.

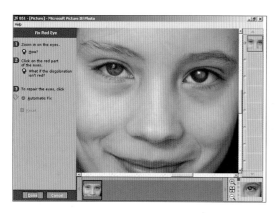

Auto Levels

Most photo-editing software programs offer an AUTO LEVELS or similarly named function that will automatically correct the COLOR, CONTRAST, and other aspects of your digital photograph.

For example, snow scenes usually come out bluish because the camera is fooled by the whiteness of the scene and accidentally underexposes the photo. The AUTO LEVEL control will usually fix this for you.

If the program has a PREVIEW option, you'll be able to see the suggested changes before committing to them.

This AUTO LEVEL command doesn't always improve the image, and it often takes it too far. So, more often than not, you'll have the best results if you do these corrections manually.

Brightness & Contrast

You can quickly improve a picture by brightening or darkening it overall with the BRIGHTNESS control. You can also increase or decrease the CONTRAST. Increasing the overall contrast makes the shadows darker and the highlights lighter. Increasing the contrast can sometimes help make a slightly blurred image look sharper.

Dodge & Burn

The overall brightness control in most programs affects the entire image. However, there will be times when you want to lighten or darken only particular parts of the picture. For example, you can DODGE a face to lighten it, or BURN a background object to make it darker and less distracting.

For the best results, adjust the SIZE of the DODGE or BURN TOOL (usually by selecting the right-sized BRUSH). Then, select the OPACITY or STRENGTH level at a low number. It's better to take several strokes at 10% OPACITY than one strong stroke at 100% OPACITY. It takes more time to get to the lightened or darkened effect that you want, but the result will be smoother and more natural looking.

STRAIGHT FROM THE CAMERA

AUTO LEVEL CORRECTION

STRAIGHT FROM THE CAMERA

BRIGHTEN OVERALL

SELECTIVE DODGING

Color Correction

It's not uncommon for your photograph to have an unwanted color cast. You may not even realize it has one until you see a corrected or improved version.

Adobe Photoshop Elements software offers a quick way to check by using the VARIATIONS command. First, it shows your original, then versions with more RED, GREEN, BLUE, CYAN (a light blue color), YELLOW, and MAGENTA (a pink color), as well as lighter or darker versions. Click on the one you like best and you're ready to go. Other software has sliding bars you move to adjust the color.

Color Modes

You can instantly change your color picture into BLACK-AND-WHITE, SEPIA (brownish), POSTER-IZED, SATURATED, DUOTONE, and more (see below.) Be sure to give the new version a different name before saving it, or the original color information will be forever lost.

Another option is selective color change, such as the background in the top right photo of the series below.

Note that when most people say, "black-and-white photo," they really mean one made up of many shades of gray (bottom left photo), not just black and white.

NORMAL

SATURATED

BACKGROUND

BLACK & WHITE

BLUE

SEPIA

Stamp or Clone

This is a great tool if want to quickly retouch your pictures. The concept is that you "rubber-stamp" one part of the picture to pick up "ink" and then stamp it down elsewhere. You can quickly cover a facial blemish in a portrait or clear out trash from a background. Random textured areas, such as grass or bushes, are often the easiest to work with. Select new "ink" often to avoid creating an unwanted pattern when you do this.

Retouching

Retouching refers to repairing or improving a photograph, such as removing blemishes from a portrait, cleaning up distracting objects from the background, toning down a bright spot, and more. There are a variety of TOOLS you might use to do this.

What to Change?

Before you start retouching, try to come up with a plan. First fix the BRIGHTNESS, CONTRAST, or COLOR because this will make the biggest, fastest improvement (as seen in versions #1 and #2 of the puppy). Try AUTO LEVELS first, but if that doesn't look perfect, use the UNDO command and then work the controls manually.

Removing distracting elements with the STAMP or CLONE tool is the next best step. Notice how the leash and the bright spots in the background were all removed. This helps focus all the attention on the dog (see pages 53 to 57 for more background hints).

Make a Best Friend Collage

Create a freaky, fun picture of your best friend and you.

1 Open a photograph in photo-editing software. Change its color properties just enough so that all the tones get a little bit bright and wacky (see page 64). Save the edited image under a slightly different name than the original.

2 Repeat step 1 three times, using the methods in this chapter to alter the look of the photos. Use painting tools, color modes, or even posterization. Check your photo-editing software for special FILTERS and BRUSH effects.

3 Save all four images under slightly different names.

4 Combine the images, making a grid out of all four. This can be done in three basic ways:

WITH A PRINTING TEMPLATE

Many different types of photo-editing, camera, and printer software offer easy templates for printing several photos on a single page. Simply pick the type of template you want (one, two, four, or more pictures per page), and then select the photos from your files.

IN WORD-PROCESSING

If you're using word-processing software, like Microsoft Word, start by opening a new document that's the size of the paper you'll print on (such as 8½ x 11-inch letter-size paper).

Insert the first photo (the commands vary by the software, but are usually named something like INSERT, GET PHOTO or FILE, or ADD OBJECT). This will create a PICTURE BOX.

You can drag this PICTURE BOX around the page with your MOUSE. You can also change its size by tugging at the corner of the box. Tugging at the corner usually just enlarges or shrinks the picture without distorting it. But in some software it can change the proportions causing distortion.

Repeat the process until all four images fit neatly on a page.

PHOTO-EDITING SOFTWARE

You can also create the four-picture combination in photo-editing software by COLLAGING the images. Open a NEW document (sometimes called a CANVAS) in the size of the paper you plan to print on.

Next add the photograph. This command varies, but it could be INSERT, IMPORT, GET PHOTO or FILE, ADD OBJECT, COLLAGE, or COPY/PASTE.

Some software treats each picture as as a separate OBJECT that you can push around the CANVAS. Adobe Elements creates LAYERS, and each layer holds one of the elements (see page 71). Either way, you can push them around the CANVAS with your MOUSE or the CURSER ARROWS.

Save the edited image under a slightly different name than the original.

5 Print the picture on heavy-weight, matte-surface paper.

6 If it's not "done," you can use markers to add new colors to the pictures. Be careful not to rub too hard with the markers. Sometimes light-colored markers can smudge or even remove some of the ink on the picture.

Stickers and ink stamps can also be added to the print. Frame your fabulous creation!

Sharpen

Most photo-editing software programs have some sort of SHARPEN tool. Unfortunately, it cannot work miracles, but it can help to improve the appearance of *slightly* unsharp images.

Be careful to use a light hand, because overly sharpened pictures get a grainy, fake look. Increasing the CONTRAST can also help create the appearance of sharpness.

Erase

You can ERASE a portion of an image to completely clear off that section. This tool is particularly useful on collages. You can overlap two photos images, and then remove parts of the first photo with the ERASE tool, so the second photo can shine through from underneath.

Painting

You can also "paint over" a photograph. Photo-editing software programs give you many choices in brushes, that vary in COLOR, SIZE, TEXTURE, and PATTERN.

Some software will give you an airbrush effect, while other will look like a watercolor brush stroke. Other programs even enable repetitive patterns that mimic wallpaper borders as you "paint."

There are lots of other artistic enhancements that you can do, depending on the software program. Read the instruction manual or just start experimenting with the various tools that the program offers. Let your imagination go wild!

Stitching Together Panoramas

Many photo-editing software programs now offer STITCHING or PANORAMA tools. Take a series of photos while you PAN the camera (see pages 58 and 59), and the software will automatically combine them for a seamless full-circle or extra-long effect (see below).

For the best results, overlap the pictures and take care to keep the camera level for all the pictures in the series.

Other Collages

Photographs can be combined as collages that are pure art or fantasy. In its simplest form, this is a grid of photos, like the envelope project outlined on page 88.

The commands to create collages vary from program to program. Look for words like COLLAGE, LAYERS, INSERT, IMPORT, GET PHOTO OR FILE, ADD OBJECT, COLLAGE, or COPY/PASTE.

Fancier methods overlap the pictures, and allow you to change the OPACITY or

TRANSPARENCY (fade the images) of the individual photos. An example is the five-photo collage we created on pages 58 and 59 to demonstrate the panning technique.

What is a Layer?

LAYERS are an advanced concept in photo-editing software programs, but if you're a computer whiz, you'll enjoy them. It's the name of a tool in Adobe Elements and Photoshop software, but it's also a concept that's found in many other programs.

The concept is that you start with the primary photo (layer 1). If you add type or another photo, you now have additional layers. Painterly brush strokes can be added as another layer. And on and on. These layers can then be deleted or duplicated at will.

What's so great about this? Afterwards you can shuffle the layers for different results, demonstrated below. A top layer can cover a lower layer. A transparent layer can allow another layer to show through. You can also alter a single layer, without affecting any of the other layers.

*RIGHT: **Layers can be stacked and shuffled. The bottom left version shows Layer 1 on top of Layer 2 on top of Layer 3. The bottom middle version has the see-through (transparent) Layer 2 on top. The last version has the opaque (solid) purple layer on top, which hides the other two.***

LAYER 1

LAYER 2

LAYER 3

LAYERS 1, 2, 3

LAYERS 2, 3, 1

LAYERS 3, 2, 1

Adding Text (Fonts)

You can add text to your pictures in most photo-editing software programs. Often, the command for adding text is a square with the letter "A" or "T" inside. This text is placed in a TEXT BOX, that can be moved around or resized, and in some cases arched, twisted, or stretched as well.

The typed letters come in different FONTS. Each FONT has a different look. Most computers come with a selection of different FONTS, but there are thousands of others you can add. Do an Internet search under the keywords "font" and "free" and you'll be surprised by how many you might find.

A FEW WORDS ON WORDS

Don't overlook the visual power of the letters themselves. Certainly, the words have meaning in terms of what they say, but they can also improve your design.

Pick your type color carefully. Yellow type may be very bold, but it can be hard to read against some background colors.

In general, dark letters are more easily read against light backgrounds, and light letters are easily read against dark backgrounds.

Some software programs allow you to warp, arc, and even twist the letters to create interesting shapes out of the words.

TYPE JUSTIFICATION

Just like in a word processing program (like Microsoft Word), you can change the JUSTIFICATION of your type.

THIS PARAGRAPH IS JUSTIFIED. All the type lines up in a neat row on the right and left sides. Sometimes it causes large gaps between the words. This can make it hard to read.

THIS PARAGRAPH IS FLUSH LEFT.
It is probably the most common choice.
The left side of the type lines up evenly and the right side ends longer or shorter.

THIS PARAGRAPH IS FLUSH RIGHT.
It leaves the ragged side on the left. It looks good lined up with something to the right.

THIS PARAGRAPH IS CENTERED.
Centered is just what it sounds like—an equal space remains on the right and left sides.

TYPE IS MEASURED IN POINT SIZE (PT.). LARGER NUMBERS MEAN BIGGER LETTERS

96pt., 48pt., 24pt., 12 pt., 6pt.

Varying the Type Face

1 THE FONT ITSELF
There are thousands of different FONTS, each of which has letters and symbols that look a little different.

2 THE POINT SIZE
Fonts are usually measured in point sizes. Larger points mean a larger size.

3 THE COLOR
You can pick any color for the letters. Make sure they're readable against the background!

4 THE SHADE
Some software lets you soften its SHADE by lightening it.

5 BACKGROUND BOX
In some software, the text is held in a box that can be colored or TRANSPARENT (COLOR NONE). A colored, black, or white box will sit as a block of color on top of the background. A TRANSPARENT box will also sit on top of the background but will be transparent except for the letters.

You can use a frame to outline this box. You can select the COLOR, WIDTH, and STYLE of this frame.

6 JUSTIFICATION
This refers to how the type lines up on the left and right sides. See page 70 for examples.

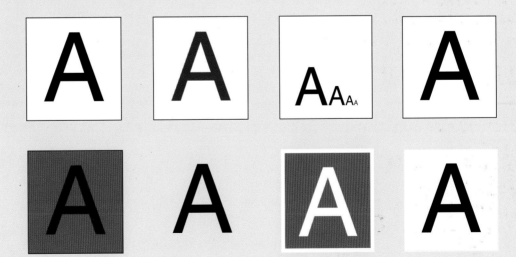

You & the Internet

If you've mastered email and surfing the Internet, you won't have any trouble taking the leap to creating your own website. Just make sure you have your parents' permission.

How Does the Internet Work?

There is not an Internet warehouse out in cyberspace where all the information on the Internet is stored. The burden of housing the information goes to individual Internet HOST companies. This HOST will "hold" all the files beonging to certain websites, and allow outside computers (like yours) to access it through an Internet address (also called an URL). That's the "www" address, which usually ends in ".COM", ".ORG", ".NET", or one of the new address endings.

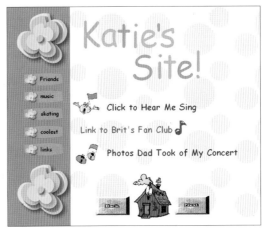

Katie's Site!

Friends
music
skating
coolest
links

Click to Hear Me Sing
Link to Brit's Fan Club
Photos Dad Took of My Concert

KID SLEUTH

MY RECENT PROJECTS

Day at the Zoo

How do planes fly?

Shark Fest!

Send me an email!

Your Own Website

It's easier than you think to create your own website, but you'll need to do it with your parent's help. You probably won't need their help figuring out how to create the site, but you'll need their input on what you should and shouldn't post.

For example, for safety reasons, never give your full name, or any information that reveals where you live or go to school. After all, everyone *you* know, knows that information already. Strangers don't need it, so you shouldn't put it out there for them to find.

What's a Host?

To get started, first have your family check with your INTERNET SERVICE PROVIDER (ISP), such as AOL, Comcast, Roadrunner, or Earthlink. Many give their subscribers a free homepage with their monthly subscription.

If the company provides this service, then it probably also offers simple online web-designing software. You just log in and start building your pages with easy-to-understand instructions. Click on a TEMPLATE, choose your color scheme, type in your text, and add pictures!

You can even add guest books (for friends to write comments), calendars, slide show galleries, and sometimes movies.

If your ISP doesn't offer webpage hosting, another option is free or inexpensive monthly hosting from an outside company. These usually base their charges on how much memory your pages take.

Emailing Pictures

Sending a picture by email is easy. You open an email in your mail software (such as Microsoft Outlook or AOL). Then click on ATTACH or INSERT, and select your photo file.

What's not so easy is resizing the picture so it's a manageable size. If it's too high a resolution, it'll take a very long time for the person who receives it to download—especially if they still use a telephone line to connect to the Internet.

It's best to save a separate, smaller email version. This is usually done in photo-editing software. Check to see if there is a special function for "web" sizing. If not, select the IMAGE SIZE (or similarly named) command. Then type in the size you want. For a small picture, choose 400x600 at 100 dpi. For a larger one, select 600x900 at 100 dpi.

You can make it even smaller by using JPEG compression (see pages 14 and 15).

Internet Safety

Try to find a web host that enables passwords. This way, potential visitors (like your friends and relatives) can type in a password you supply to view the site, but strangers can't. If your internet provider doesn't offer this service, your parents can register with an internet hosting site that does.

Some kid-friendly hosting sites include:

- Yahoo Geocities (www.geocities.yahoo.com)
- My Family (www.myfamily.com)
- My School (www.myschoolonline.com)

Remember that anything you post on the Internet is accessible by the general public unless you take very special (and complicated) steps. In the same way you wouldn't give a stranger your phone number or address, don't give away the same information on the web!

Never post anything without approval of your parents.

MORE INFORMATION

Check out my other book, *Making Family Websites* (Lark Books) if you want more information on building your own website. It will help you get started quickly, and covers many different issues, from safety to design techniques. Creating a website is a great project for the whole family!

BELOW: CLIPART *is a source of fun graphics that you can use as click-links on your website. These* LINKS *take the viewer from one page of your site to the next*.

Easy Web Pages

Templates let you build websites in just minutes!

It only took a few minutes to create each of these pages with the online software provided by hosts like Homestead, Lycos-Tripod, and Yahoo-Geocities.

You could also design your pages in easy software that you buy from a store and then upload them to the HOST of your choice.

NEWSLETTERS

PARTY INVITES

DIARIES & BLOGS

FAMILY TREE

PET PAGES

GUEST BOOKS

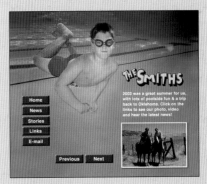

FAMILY SITE

6

Printing Pizzazz

Once you take great digital pictures, you can print them in different sizes, or turn them into greeting cards, magnets, or creative art and crafts projects.

Print Your Pictures

Printing your pictures at home is usually done with an inkjet printer. Most printers connect to your computer with a cord or other method. Software that comes with the printer insures that it works properly. When you initiate a PRINT command, a print MENU usually pops up that walks you through the process.

A few printers have "stand-alone" capability, meaning they don't need a computer to function. Just load in a memory card or stick or attach your camera (via cord, INFRARED, or a DOCK) and print.

Forget selling cupcakes to raise money at a bake sale! With this kind of printer, all you need is a power source, and you can make prints from your digital camera and sell them then and there!

Choose a Printer

There are numerous things to consider before picking a printer. Most home color printers are inkjet printers—but all inkjets are not the same!

First of all, the printer must be able to work with your computer's operating system (such as Windows XP or Mac OSX), and have the right kind of connection (such as USB or FIREWIRE port).

Plain old four-color printers are nice and economical. But to get the best photo-realistic colors (prints that look like photos from the store), you'll want a printer with five or more colors. Also, look for a printer with a separate black cartridge if this printer is doing double duty for letters, reports, and other non-picture documents. This lets you replace the black color, instead of having to trash ALL the colors when just the black runs out.

The average printer can print letter and legal sized prints, but it may have trouble with extra small or large sizes. Some high-end printers can print banners and rolls for pictures a yard long.

Consider the thickness and weight of the paper that the printer can handle. This is especially true if you want to use some of the specialty paper described on pages 82 and 83. Even if a printer can physically push the paper through its rollers, if it's not designed to use it, the inks may smear.

So-called snapshot printers are very convenient for beginning photographers. They are designed to make photo prints just like those you get from a one-hour lab or the store. They are very easy to use. Usually the paper and inks are in one easy cartridge.

The newest generation of printers offer archival and water-resistant inks. This means they'll last a lot longer without fading, and they'll hold up to smudging and spills better than traditional inkjet prints.

And then there are the biggest consideration: price. Remember it's not just the price of *buying* the printer. Find out how much the ink costs, and about how many prints you can make per cartridge.

Don't worry. If you don't want to invest in a printer right now, consider the options in the sidebar on page 81.

Make a Print

You can use all sorts of different software to make perfect prints quickly and easily.

Some of the newer printers can automatically tell what type of paper you are using and set up your prints automatically. However, if your printer doesn't do this, or it doesn't recognize the paper you're using, you have a few options.

1 THE EASIEST METHOD: PRINTING SOFTWARE

Your printer or camera probably came with some software that makes printing easy by using TEMPLATES. These are preset patterns that place the picture (or pictures) in the right place on the page, so they print well.

That might not sound hard with a full-page photo, but what about when you want to make a sheet of nine wallet-size (2x3-inch) pictures? Or if you're using special pre-cut or SCORED paper for borderless prints?

Usually this software will show a gallery of all the pictures in a particu-lar FOLDER. You just click on the one you want, select the print or paper/media type and go. Often you can rotate the picture or make simple image enhancements like cropping, color, or red-eye correction.

If you don't find this software, check the original printer software install CD, or go to the manufacturer's web-site. You can also download Kodak's free version, called EasyShare, off their site at www.kodak.com.

You can also purchase software, such as Film Factory, which will help you organize and print your photographs.

2 PHOTO-EDITING SOFTWARE

Many PHOTO-EDITING software programs have photo printing TEMPLATES. Some simply position one, two, four or more photos on one sheet of paper. Others are designed for particular papers.

Some provide fantastic graphic TEMPLATES for collages and more.

Adobe Photoshop Elements and Adobe Photoshop printing templates can be found under the commands FILE→AUTOMATE→PICTURE PACKAGE.

MGI PhotoSuite offers many options under their print MENU, including PRINT MULTIPLES.

Canon's ZoomBrowser Ex offers templates for up to 20 pictures per page.

In Microsoft Picture It, select the PICK A DESIGN command for some fun templates. Just add your pictures to make funny money with your face, fake magazine covers, trading cards, and even an ID for your secret club.

3 WORD-PROCESSING SOFTWARE

If you don't have a matching printing template for your needs, you can do it manually in word-processing software. Paper with pre-cut shapes (like CD stickers) come with instructions on where to place the pictures on the page, so it matches the paper.

Manually placing the photos is also a good solution when you have small or odd-shaped pictures (such as finger-nail decals or tattoos), because you might be able to fit more on a page than with a printing template.

To start, OPEN a NEW document in WORD-PROCESSING software like Microsoft Word. If you're using a paper size other than LETTER ($8\frac{1}{2}$ x 11 inches), select the commands PAGE SETUP→PAPER and enter the measurements.

Use the commands INSERT→PICTURE→ FROM FILE to place the first photo. You'll need to tell the computer which photo to use, by SCROLLING through your FILE FOLDERS (such as MY PICTURES) until the right file shows up.

If you're matching measurement instructions (such as for pre-cut CD stickers), select VIEW→RULERS so you can place the photo precisely. Then DRAG the photo so that a top corner is in the right place. Then tug at the corner of the PICTURE BOX with the MOUSE make it larger or smaller as needed.

Careful! Pulling on the sides of the image can stretch or squash the picture as it makes it larger or smaller. But tugging on the corner will keep it proportional (undistorted).

Repeat the process to add as many pictures as you'd like using this method. Then print the document!

Get Good Results

Getting good results with your printer is something of an art form. If you're getting poor results there are a few ways you can make quick improvements.

Check your paper. Use paper made for inkjet printers. Regular copy paper will never produce great photo results. The glossier the surface of the paper, the more your prints will look like "real" prints from a photofinishing lab.

Check your inks. If they're not a major brand, they may not be high enough quality to make good prints.

Check your image size or resolution. For good prints, you'll need a DPI (dots per inch) measurement of *at least* 150dpi at the size you're printing. That means for every inch of print you make, there must be over 150 pixels (and preferably more) for good results. Anything less, and the picture might not look good.

To check, open the picture in PHOTO-EDITING SOFTWARE and hit the IMAGE SIZE (or similarly named) command. It will list a size in inches or pixels (4x6 inches or 600x700 pixels for example). It will also give a DPI. If the DPI is listed at 75 (half of 150), then the printable size of the picture is half of what is listed when you view IMAGE SIZE menu. *(Math again!)* If it's too small, you may have to print it smaller for good results. Using a higher resolution will help next time.

Inkjet Inks

Because inkjet inks are designed for white papers, they are not OPAQUE. (Opaque means it blocks the light, like the ink from those metallic pens). On white paper, it's no problem. But switch to clear labels or decals and it will look dull or invisible over a dark or colored background.

Don't despair—use it as an advantage. Check out the party place holders we make on page 92. The pictures of the guests were put on transparent decal material and then transferred to colored construction paper. The result? The tone of the paper can be seen through the picture for an artistic result.

Fabric Transfer Materials

T-shirt transfer or so-called "iron-on" transfer material isn't just iron-on anymore! Not all fabrics can handle the heat of an iron, so fabric transfer material is now available for cold transfer. This is great for crafts projects, such as the change purse on page 84.

Before buying transfer material, decide what you'll be applying it to. Not just because of the fabric's heat sensitivity, but also its color. Most t-shirt transfer material for example is clear (TRANSPARENT). This is great if you put it on a white or light shirt, because the only "background" becomes the shirt itself.

However, try this on your favorite black t-shirt and the image may seem to disappear (see examples above). You'll need to use transfer material made for dark materials. This is printed on white, so trim the picture very carefully after printing it to avoid white edges (unless you *want* white edges!)

Printing Options

If your don't like your results, some printers may give you the opportunity to adjust the color. Others work with sophisticated color-matching software (like ColorSync) that helps match what you see on your monitor to the print.

Without either of these, you may have to go back into photo-editing software and adjust the color of your digital photo in order to improve the print.

Once you select the PRINT command, on most printers a print MENU will pop up giving you some of these choices:

LEFT: *Regular fabric transfer sheets look good on white, but look faded on colored or dark t-shirts*. *For brighter images on dark fabric use transfer paper designed specifically for dark fabrics*. *You'll need to trim the image before transferring to avoid white edges*.

Note that you can get both iron-on and cold transfer varieties.

1 NUMBER OF COPIES
Paper is expensive. Always select just one for your first print, to make sure it's perfect before printing off more copies.

2 PHOTO SIZES
Depending on your printer, you can print from small individual 4 x 6 prints, through standard letter-size (8½ x 11inch), and sometimes larger. Extremely large or small choices are usually only offered on expensive printers.

3 PAPER ORIENTATION
Do you want it to print vertically like a normal letter (also called PORTRAIT mode), or sideways so it's wider than it's long (also called LANDSCAPE mode)? Most paper has a front (for the ink) and a back (a different texture not intended for ink).

4 PAPER TYPE
Pages 82 and 83 list many of the different papers available. The printer may alter its speed based on the type of media. Some take longer to dry, so they could smear if they are run through the rollers

too fast. Likewise, economy or draft prints are done fast (and sometimes with less ink) to save time and money.

5 INK LEVELS & CLEANING
A few printers may ask you about INK LEVELS, or if you want to CLEAN HEADS. If your printer has not been used for a while, click YES. Switch to cheap paper for this.

6 WHICH PRINTER?
Finally, you may be asked to select which printer to use, if you have more than one set up on the computer. In some cases, you may need to unplug one printer from the computer, and replace it with the photo printer.

CAN'T PRINT AT HOME?

■ Go to your local photo-finishing lab. Most have digital printing services.

■ Look for a Kodak or other self-service printing kiosk. They're in a lot of grocery stores and pharmacies. Insert your memory card or CD and print!

■ You can also upload your digital pictures to an online photofinisher. They will make galleries for you, which you can share with friends. You can also edit and improve the pictures online. Two top companies include www.shutterfly.com or www.kodakgalleries.com.

You can also enhance these images with RED-EYE correction, CROPPING, BORDERS and more. And then you can turn them into prints of different sizes, professional-looking greeting cards, calendars, bound books, and more.

Paper Types

The paper (also called media) you use could be the single most important decision you make when it comes to good prints. Regular copy paper simply isn't made for inkjet inks. The results are dull and blurry, because the inks bleed together.

At the very least, select light-weight inkjet paper for letters and school reports. If you're going to include photographs, switch to photo-quality paper in a letter weight (20 to 27lb.) For photos that feel real, switch to the thick photo-weight, photo-quality papers.

Paper thickness is described in terms of how many pounds a certain number of pages weigh. Therefore a lower number (like 20lb.) will be a lot thinner than a high number (like 80lb.). It will also be a lot cheaper to buy.

REGULAR PRINTS ARE GREAT, BUT THERE'S MUCH MORE!

- **DRAFT (ECONOMY) PAPERS**: Use cheaper papers to clean the printer heads, or to check the placement of a photo. (Print it on the cheap paper, then lay it against the expensive paper and hold it up to a light or the window to see how it lines up with pre-cut shapes or greeting card paper.)

- **PHOTO-QUALITY**: This term is confusing. On some brands it means the paper is thick and heavy like a real photo print. However on other brands, it can just mean that it is thin letter-weight paper that has a surface that is good for inkjet photos.

- **PHOTO-WEIGHT**: These are heavier papers that look and feel like the prints you used to get when you had your film processed.

- **PRE-CUT OR PERFORATED**: Some photo-weight paper has one or more perforated (easy to tear) or pop-out (pre-cut) shapes on each page. This lets you easily print borderless pictures. Just make the print area a little bigger than the cut-out. When you pop it out, it will be borderless.

- **ROLLS**: A few printers can handle paper rolls. The primary use is to print the huge panoramic photos that you can make by stitching together several pictures (see page 70).

- **GREETING CARDS**: You can make greeting cards that look as good (or better!) than those from the store. Special greeting card media comes with matching envelopes, and is SCORED to fold nicely after you print it. Usually the part that becomes the front of the card is a photo-weight glossy paper.

LEFT: *Special decal paper lets you make rub-on temporary tattoos. You need to print them backward (flip) to make them look correct when applied.*

ABOVE: *You can apply fabric transfer sheets to almost any fabric, including quilting squares. Choose iron-on transfers for cotton and other fabrics that can be ironed. Choose cold-transfer versions for all other fabrics.*

▦ **FABRIC TRANSFER**: In the old days, this was called iron-on material. But now cold transfer versions are available for fabrics that can't be ironed. Choose the right types for light-colored or dark-colored fabrics (see page 80).

▦ **ADHESIVE LABELS**: Mailing address label paper is great for making your own stickers, as well as craft projects. Usually they are pre-cut into small labels for envelopes, but full uncut sheets are available. White labels will have the boldest colors. Clear labels are great for colored papers, when you want the color to shine though (see page 92). Make sure you buy the type made for inkjet printers.

▦ **MAGNETS**: This type of paper comes with a thin magnetic backing. You can purchase it with pre-cut shapes (including circles), or full sheets that you cut yourself. Alternately, you can print on regular photo paper, and then apply adhesive-backed magnet stickers.

▦ **TATTOOS & FINGERNAIL DECALS**: This type of paper is a two-part process. First print on the special paper. Then rub it onto a second peel-off adhesive paper to make a tattoo sandwich. Place it next to your skin or nail, wet the back, and carefully peel away the backing!

The tattoo will be "backward," so if you're printing words you'll need to use the ROTATE→FLIP HORIZONTALLY commands in photo-editing software so it will print backward (and look right when applied).

▦ **FUZZY PAPERS**: Perfect for the doll house! This ink-jet paper is actually fuzzy!

▦ **SHRINK ART PLASTICS**: Print a picture on this clear plastic, put it in the oven for a few seconds, and it shrinks into a thick hard plastic that's great for jewelry, ornaments, and crafts.

▦ **BUSINESS PAPERS**: Look in the business section of the store too! I bet you can come up with some projects that use preprinted newsletter, brochure, and business card papers, as well as clear plastic overhead transparency materials.

7 Fun Ideas & Projects

Armed with your digital camera, an inkjet printer, and a few supplies, you can create a wide variety of crafts. Start with these and springboard to your own ideas!

Change Your Change Purse!

Use t-shirt transfer paper to *change* a change purse into something really cool. Start by selecting a fabric purse and some fabric transfer paper. Some transfer papers are done cold, but others require a heated iron. If heat is required, make sure the purse's fabric won't melt!

You can either scan the coins (see pages 22 and 23) or photograph them with your digital camera.

For the latter, spread loose change over a clean area such as a sheet or floor. Try not to have any blank spaces between the coins. Do it near a window or in a fairly bright area so you won't need a flash, because the flash could cause glare off the metal coins.

Transfer the picture to your computer and save it. Measure the area of your purse to be covered. Use a PRINTING TEMPLATE, WORD-PROCESSING software, or PHOTO-EDITING software to print the picture (see pages 78 and 79).

You may want to do a print on regular paper first, to check the size before using the expensive transfer paper. When you have it right, print the transfer paper, trim it carefully and apply it to the purse following the instructions that come with the paper.

Me, Myself & I Bookplates

You'll never lose another book if you're the star of your own fancy bookplates. It's incredibly easy—just print a great picture on adhesive label paper that's made for inkjet printers. Pick the type that's a single sheet, instead of a lot of little pre-cut labels. That way you can make the bookplate any size you want, and just trim it with scissors. If it's about 4 x 4 inches, you can fit four of them on one sheet of paper.

How did we make this really wild bookplate? It took a lot of fancy photo software footwork, but it was worth it. Every software program has different names for their commands, but most can do this:

■ Take a photo of yourself (see page 29 for information on self-portraits) and a photo of a book.

■ OPEN the picture of yourself in PHOTO-EDITING software. Then OPEN the photo of the book. Use the CUT and PASTE commands (it could be called INSERT, IMPORT, GET PICTURE, ADD OBJECT, or COLLAGE) to add the book to your portrait.

■ You may have to fiddle with its SIZE until it looks right in your hand. And you may want to ROTATE it. In some software you can do it in the now combined picture collage. In other software, you'll have to start over and RESIZE and ROTATE the book picture before copying it. (See page 74 for information on resizing).

■ Next, duplicate the self-portrait, and paste it into the book. Again you may need to play with the SIZE and ROTATION.

■ In some software, you can change the TRANSPARENCY or OPACITY of the parts or LAYERS of the image (see page 69). Here, the OPACITY of the portrait in the book was changed to make it see-through.

■ Add other creative touches like CLIPART flowers or a fancy photo-edge BORDER, such as a string of candy beads.

■ Save the collage as a new digital photo under a different name (so it doesn't OVERWRITE your self-portrait). Print it using the instructions on pages 78 and 79.

Simple Stationery

The simplest photo stationary uses pictures to make a border around the writing space on a piece of paper. You can mix your own photos with CLIPART cartoons, borders, and words.

Letter-Weight Papers

For the best results, use papers made for ink-jet printing. You don't need the glossy, expensive photo-weight papers. These will be hard to fold anyway. Instead pick something in the 20 to 27lb. range.

The instructions will vary depending on what software you use.

In Photo Software

You can design your stationery in most photo-editing software, such as Adobe Photoshop Elements, MGI PhotoSuite, Microsoft Picture It, Scansoft PhotoFactory, and Ulead PhotoImpact.

Remember that you can use photos, as well as other tools like the PAINTBRUSH (which made the blue stripes in the example shown below). Better software gives you hundreds of choices in BRUSH types and size, as well as COLOR, SHADE, and the PATTERN it makes.

The yellow diamond shapes were made by creating an AUTO SHAPE and then filling or painting it with color. Some programs have special FILTERS or BRUSH effects to add texture or patterns to these shapes. A diamond shape was used for the yellow at the top of the page.

In Word Software

You can also design your stationery in word processing software, such as Microsoft Word. To do this, you will have to first gather all your elements in photo software (see above), and select INSERT→PICTURE→FROM FILE to place the elements. The WordArt function in some versions of Microsoft Word allows you to create crazy type as well.

Last Step

The last step is easy! Print the picture following the steps on pages 78 and 79. Use scissors to follow edges of a picture or shape (such as the yellow diamonds) for a special look. Crafts scissors that make a scalloped or jagged edge are also fun.

Transparency Option

Some photo software programs let you change the TRANSPARENCY or OPACITY of the picture or a LAYER or portion of the picture. This is great for stationery, because you can print a whole page picture at 10% or 20% of the original OPACITY, and it will show up like a ghost image or a background design. You can still write on top of it, and the words are easy to read because the picture is so faint.

Dear Grandma,
Thanks for the birthday gift!

HINT!!

Have a lot of people to write to, and the same information to deliver? Type it in word-processing software and select a font that looks like handwriting for a personal look.

Easiest Envelope

After an awesome vacation, write a letter to a friend and tuck it in an envelope that looks like a postcard. The easiest way to make one is to start with a real envelope, and run it through the printer. But you can only do this if your printer can handle the thickness and small size of an envelope.

If your printer or word-processing software has an envelope TEMPLATE, you're home-free. Instead of typing in an address, INSERT a picture. In common software like Microsoft Word, select INSERT PHOTO. Then tug at the edges so it fills most of the space.

Make sure that pulling at the edge does not distort the image by stretching or scrunching it. Different software has different ways to enlarge the picture—some enlarge it proportionately, so it does not distort. If you find it distorting, you may have to check the instruction manual.

You'll need to know if your printer feeds the envelope in the long or short way. You may have to ROTATE the image, so it will look right when viewed normally (sideways or LANDSCAPE).

Without an envelope TEMPLATE, you'll need to be more creative.

Open a NEW document and pick a command called PAGE SETUP or DOCUMENT SETUP, or similar. Then click on your envelope size. Click LANDSCAPE mode if you want it to be right-side-up on the envelope. You may also have to select CUSTOM paper size in the printer menu (see pages 78 and 79) if it doesn't list your exact envelope size.

Most printers will leave a small border on the edges of the envelope. Check and see if you printer MENU has a BORDERLESS option. If not, you can always use a magic marker to change this blank edge into a fancy decorative border.

Picture Hint

The final goal is to make an envelope that will still look good after you add stamps, and the "to" and "from" addresses. A photograph with a relatively simple area in the center for the address is important, so the post office can read the writing!

Use a black pen over light areas, and a silver or gold opaque metallic pen over dark areas. If all else fails, add a white sticker label.

Fold Your Own Envelope

It's not hard to make your own envelope. All you need is a design TEMPLATE (a pattern) and some glue. The trick is to print the paper first, then cut out the shape, fold it just right, and glue the flaps together (as shown in the five photos at left).

Like so many of these projects, you can make the face collage shown here in either a WORD-PROCESSING program like Microsoft Word, or a PHOTO-EDITING software program.

In this example, we have six photos that are repeated over and over again. You can use any pictures you want, and as many variations as inspires you.

Before starting, you may want to make smaller versions of these pictures so the document won't become too large in FILE SIZE when they're all combined. A good choice would be to RESIZE them to 1x1-inch size at 150dpi. Be sure to give them a new name, like "envelope1" and "envelope2" so you don't lose the higher resolution version. See pages 11 and 12 for more details on RESIZING.

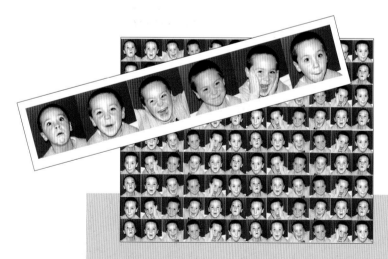

1 Combine mini photos to make one big page of pictures.

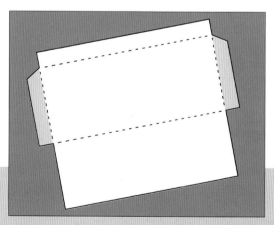

2 Carefully peel apart a real envelope and use it to make a template, or scan and enlarge this one.

In Word Software

In a WORD-PROCESSING SOFTWARE such as Microsoft Word, start with a NEW letter-size (8½ x 11-inch) document. Use PAGE SETUP to turn it sideways (LANDSCAPE mode). INSERT a photo. Tug at the edges of the photo box to make it the size you want. Then use your MOUSE to DRAG it into the top right corner. Repeat with all six pictures. Then use SELECT ALL and COPY and PASTE the group. Do it over and over again until you fill the whole page.

In Photo Software

In PHOTO-EDITING SOFTWARE, you'll be doing the same thing (repeating the photographs), except it's called COLLAGE or LAYER. The commands vary depending on the software, but usually it is INSERT, COLLAGE, GET PHOTO or FILE, ADD OBJECT, or COPY/PASTE.

Envelope Templates

Use the pattern shown on the previous page to make your envelope pattern. You can scan it, en-large it to fit letter-sized paper, and then print it.

Another option is to carefully peel apart a real envelope. A little steam from a tea kettle or steam iron will loosen the glue without making the paper too soggy. But be careful not to burn yourself in the process.

You may be tempted to print on the highest quality glossy photo paper. However, because it's so thick, it may not fold well. Instead, pick a lighter weight (and less expensive) paper, such as 27lb. photo-quality paper.

Lay your envelope pattern over the newly printed paper, and cut out the notches. Fold the print along the dotted lines.

If you want the pictures on the outside of the envelope, fold the blank sides towards each other. For a secret inside surprise, fold the picture side inward. This will create the photos on the inside of the envelope.

Glue where indicated on the template (the light gray areas). Once the letter is finished and loaded into the envelope, glue or tape the final flap.

3 Print the multi-picture and then use the pattern at left to trace and cut the right shape.

4 Fold and glue the envelope. If the design is too busy for a readable address, use a white sticker label.

Peek-Out Cards

Surprise your friend or a family member with a card that stars their face! You can use card stock or poster board to make the folding card shape. Use a size that, when folded, will fit into an envelope.

Use a large die-cut paper punch to make holes in the front of the card. These punches are available at crafts stores, and come in a variety of patterns and sizes.

You can make multiple holes or just one. If you do just one, it usually looks best if the hole is a little higher than the center of the card (as shown in the example at right).

Measure the size of the hole the punch makes. You'll be printing a picture that's slightly larger than this hole.

Open up a word-processing software program or a printing TEMPLATE, and INSERT a photo and then make the PHOTO BOX slightly bigger than the size of the hole punch. Put several on the page, if you have multiple holes or plan to make several cards.

Print the page on a sheet of uncut self-adhesive label paper. You don't want the type that is pre-cut into a lot of little labels. If your card is white, white adhesive paper will look best. Choose clear adhesive label paper if you want the color of the paper to shine through the photo (see pages 92 and 93).

With the card closed, lightly trace the outline of the hole onto the writing space (the inside of the card) with a pencil. This is where you'll place the photo. Since the picture is slightly larger than the hole, it will cover these lines.

Peel off the adhesive backing and stick the image to the card—covering the pencil outline you made.

Add rubber stamps, stickers, glitter, or hand-drawn designs to the card.

Surprise Birthday Party Invite

The hardest part of this project will be to get a sneaky picture of the person who will be surprised with a party. Try surprising them by hiding and then jumping up to take a picture. Or trick them by telling them you need to take a funny picture of a scared or surprised person for a school project.

Next photograph a door. Make sure you include part of the wall and door frame as well. Add balloons or party banners for even more fun.

If your camera has a zoom lens, zoom it to the TELE or T setting, and walk pretty far away to take the picture. This will cause the least distortion. If you shoot close up with the WIDE or W setting, the door may look bowed. You may have the best luck with a front door, rather than an inside door, because you can step back farther away from it for the TELE picture.

Use PLAYBACK mode to make sure your door is as straight as possible.

Once you have your pictures the rest is easy. Make a card by folding colored paper and trimming it to a size that will smoothly fit into an envelope.

If you want to get fancy, you can use a word-processing program to first print the invitation message on the inside of the card. Select a letter document and use PAGE SETUP to make it landscape (sideways), Then select a RIGHT MARGIN of 1.0 inches, and a LEFT MARGIN of 6.5 inches. The result will be text only on the right side, so it looks correct when folded!

Using the printing instructions on pages 78 and 79, print the photos onto glossy photoweight paper. Both pictures (the door and the person) will probably fit on one page, so you can save time and paper printing them together (see photo below). Just make sure the person is small enough to fit inside the door.

Put the photo of the door on a piece of cardboard. Using a ruler as a guide, carefully cut around three sides of the door with the craft knife. Leave the hinged side intact. This will allow the door to open.

On the front of the card, first glue the photo of the person. Then, apply glue to the back of the door print, but not on the folded door itself. Place this over the person. When the recipient pulls open the door, they will see the birthday girl or boy.

Place Cards & Gift Tags

Help your friends find their places at your next party by finding their faces!

You'll need to plan ahead and shoot pictures of all your friends. Use the portrait techniques described on pages 43 to 45 for good head-and-shoulder images.

In a photo-editing software program, you can also "paint" over the photos. Try drawing fun, colorful hats on each person. Use several different colors in each hat for the best results.

Most WORD-PROCESSING, PHOTO-EDITING, and PRINTING software will provide a PRINTING TEMPLATE for wallet-sized (2x3-inch) prints. Just indicate which photo files you want printed, and the program will layout a page full of them. If you don't have a template, use the instructions on pages 78 and 79 and create this page in WORD-PROCESSING software, like Microsoft Word.

Print the page of photos on clear adhesive-backed label paper. Look for the variety that is one piece, without pre-cut mini-labels. Trim away the non-picture parts around each face.

Cut colored card stock into interesting shapes. Then apply the face label. Because you're using clear labels, some of the color of the card will show through the photos. Add additional decorations in the form of stickers, rubber stamps, or markers.

If the tag is being used for a gift, punch a hole in the bottom and attach a ribbon. For place cards, use clothes pin to stand up the place tags.

Pet Portraits

The basic concept to this project is to bend a wire coat hanger into a square shape, cover it with fabric, and decorate it with hot or cold t-shirt transfer material.

Begin by taking a good digital shot of your pet. Then select some pet-oriented objects like biscuits, squeak toys or a collar and scan them (see pages 22 and 23). Look for free funny CLIPART as well. (CLIPART is available on CDs, as well as for free from some websites. Do an Internet search under the words "free clipart" to find sources.)

You can COLLAGE the pet picture with the other objects to make one photo. Or you can print and transfer them separately.

Reshape the hanger into a rectangle, and measure the size. You want your picture (or pictures) to be under this size. Print the picture on the transfer paper.

Cut out all the iron-on pieces with the scissors. Cut a piece of patterned fabric a little smaller than the opening in the hanger. Transfer the pet portrait onto this fabric. Be sure to follow the iron-on paper's instructions for how to do it.

To make the frame, lay the reshaped hanger onto a larger piece of canvas, and cut the canvas 2 inches bigger than the outside edges of the hanger. Round off the corners and cut a few lines at the corners so it will wrap around smoothly.

Turn the canvas face down and center the hanger in the middle of the canvas. Cover the hanger's handle with a paper towel. Spray the outside 2 inches of the canvas with spray adhesive, or you can apply white glue. Neatly turn the edges over the hanger. Wrap the hanger's handle with a piece of yarn.

Glue the fabric with the picture onto the canvas frame. For added flare, cut a triangle of bandanna fabric. Iron on some small pictures. Tie a knot in two ends of the triangle.

WHAT YOU NEED

- Digital photo of your pet
- Scans, digital photos, or clipart of pet-related objects such as toys
- Wire coat hanger
- 12x18-inch piece of lightweight canvas
- 8x10-inch scrap of patterned cotton fabric.
- Bandanna material
- Spray adhesive or white glue
- Iron-on transfer paper (hot or cold transfer depending on the fabric)
- Very sharp scissors
- 12-inch piece of yarn

Glossary

AUTOFLASH: The camera's automated flash mode. It usually fires the flash in low-light situations.

AUTOFOCUS: The camera automatically focuses on what it thinks is the main subject (on most cameras this is whatever is in the center of the frame).

AUTOLEVEL: A software tool that tries to correct and improve a picture in one step.

BITMAP (BMP): A picture file format common on the Internet.

BLUR: A software filter that can add different types of blur to all or part of a photo.

BRIGHTNESS: A software tool that can lighten or darken a digital picture.

BROWSER: Software program that allows you to access the Internet, such as Internet Explorer and Netscape.

BURN: A software tool that lets you darken a portion of a digital picture. Also, when you burn a CD, you are recording information on it.

CLIPART: Digital drawings, animation, or photos that you can buy or get for free.

CLONE: *See* stamp.

COMPOSITION: An art term for how a picture is designed.

COMPRESSION: A way of reducing the file size of a computer file (such as a digital picture). The JPEG picture format can be compressed to small sizes.

CONTRAST: A software tool that makes shadows darker and highlights brighter.

DELETE: Permanently erase a file or picture. When clearing all pictures from a memory card or memory stick it is sometimes called format or reformat.

DIGITAL ZOOM: A camera feature that makes your subject look closer. This is done electronically rather than with the lens. *See* optical zoom.

DIGITIZE: To turn a film image into a computer-friendly format.

DOCK: Some cameras have a special dish that you place your camera on to download photos to the computer (instead of a cord).

DODGE: A software tool that can lighten a portion of a digital picture.

DOWNLOAD: To transfer pictures from your camera to computer, or Internet to computer. Also called upload.

DPI (DOTS PER INCH): A measurement that defines the number of dots in a print. Often used interchangeably with PPI.

DUOTONE: Basically a black-and-white photo that also has a secondary color.

DV (DIGITAL VIDEO): Movies that are saved in a computer file format rather than on videotape or film.

EQUIVALENT ISO: This figure indicates a camera's low-light capability, with a higher number being better. See pages 29–30.

FILE SIZE: How much memory space a file (such as a digital picture) takes to store in a camera or computer's memory. High resolution pictures have a bigger file size than low resolution pictures.

FILL FLASH: A flash mode that fires the camera's built-in or accessory flash to add some front lighting to the subject.

FILTER: In photo-editing software, filters, such as sharpen or blur, are used to make alterations and enhancements to a digital photo. On an SLR camera it is an accessory that attaches to the lens.

FIREWIRE: A type of port to connect computers, cameras, scanners, etc., so they can transfer files between them.

FIXED-FOCUS: A camera that can't autofocus.

FLIP: A software command that reverses a photo, like a mirror reflection. *See* rotate.

FOCUS LOCK: The autofocusing on most cameras is very center-oriented. focus lock enables you to take off-centered pictures that are properly focused.

FONT: Another word for typeface. TIMES and HELVETICA are common fonts.

FORMAT: *See* delete.

GIF: A picture file format common on the Internet. Common with clipart.

GIGABYTE (GB): A measurement of file size. A gigabyte is 1000 times larger than a megabyte (MB).

HIGH RESOLUTION: *See* resolution.

HOST: The company that "houses" a website, allowing visitors to access it.

INSERT: A software command that adds a photo or type to a picture or document.

INTERNET SERVICE PROVIDER (ISP): The company that enables you to access the Internet from your computer.

JPEG: A picture format that is a good choice for digital photos.

LAYERS: A software design capability that allows pictures and type to be stacked and shuffled so they overlap in different ways.

LOW RESOLUTION: *See* resolution.

MACRO: Close-up shooting capability.

MEDIA: Another word for specialty inkjet papers and materials.

MEGABYTE (MB): A measurement of file size. A high resolution photo may be over 2 MB.

MEGAPIXEL: 1,000,000 pixels. Often used to indicate the resolution of a camera.

MEMORY CARDS OR STICKS: Removable devices onto which your digital camera records pictures. They can be erased and reused over and over again. Cards with more MB can hold more pictures before they are full.

MP3: A file format for digital sound.

OPACITY: Software allows you to make an entire picture or a software tool (like stamp) solid (opaque) or see-through (transparent). 100% opacity is solid, while a lower percentages become more transparent.

OPTICAL ZOOM: A camera feature that makes your subject look closer. This is done optically by zooming the lens from wide to tele. *See* digital zoom.

PANNING: A camera technique that helps you get sharper images, especially of moving subjects. See pages 58–59 for details.

PIXEL: A single picture element that, when combined with others, creates a digital photograph.

PLAYBACK: Reviewing pictures on the camera's monitor.

PLUG-AND-PLAY: A camera, scanner, or software that's so easy to use, you don't even need to read the instruction manual.

PORT: A place on your computer, camera, or scanner where you can connect it to another device. USB and firewire do this with cords. It can also be done with a wireless connection.

PPI (PIXELS PER INCH): A way to state a pictures resolution in terms of how densely the pixels are packed (for example, *there are 300 per inch,* or 300 ppi).

PRINTING TEMPLATE: A pre-designed page that helps you quickly print multiple photos on one sheet of paper.

RESOLUTION: An expression of how many pixels make up a digital image. More pixels (higher resolution) means more quality but larger file sizes. *See* dpi and ppi.

ROTATE: A software command that turns or flips (reverses) a picture.

SCANNER: A machine that turns a print, film or flat artwork into a digital picture.

SCSI: An older, slower type of port to connect computers, cameras, scanners, etc., so they can transfer files between them.

SHARPEN: A photo-editing software function that can help improve sharpness of slightly soft images.

SLR CAMERA: A single-lens reflex camera, often associated with professional photography. Most SLRs offer interchangeable lenses and advanced accessories.

STAMP: A software retouching tool that copies or clones one part of an image, so you copy or stamp it elsewhere. Especially helpful for covering blemishes or background distractions.

TELE: A lens setting that makes the subject look closer than it actually is (not unlike binoculars).

TEMPLATE: *See* printing template.

TIFF: A picture file format used mostly by professionals.

TRANSPARENCY: *See* opacity.

TYPEFACE: *See* font.

UPLOAD: *See* download.

USB: A type of PORT to connect computers, cameras, scanners, etc., so they can transfer files between them.

VIEWFINDER: A viewing window that you bring up to your eye and look through to compose pictures.

WORLD WIDE WEB (WWW): A term that originally referred to the commercial sector of the Internet but is now synonymous with the Internet as a whole.

WIDE: A zoom lens setting that gives you a wider view of the scene (more included from right to left and top to bottom) than a TELE lens setting.

WIRELESS: A type of PORT to connect computers, cameras, scanners, etc., so they can transfer files between them. Unlike USB or firewire, it does not require any cords.

ZOOM: A type of lens that allows you to zoom from a WIDE view of the scene to a closer look at your subject (tele).

Metric Conversion Chart

½ inch = 1.3 cm
1 inch = 2.5 cm
2 inches = 5.1 cm
3 inches = 7.6 cm
4 inches = 10.2 cm
5 inches = 12.7 cm
8½ inches = 21.6 cm
11 inches = 27.9 cm

Index